VISIONARIES

HUAWEI STORIES

TIAN TAO
YIN ZHIFENG

Published by
LID Publishing Limited
The Record Hall, Studio 204,
16-16a Baldwins Gardens,
London EC1N 7RJ, UK

524 Broadway, 11th Floor, Suite 08-120,
New York, NY 10012, US

info@lidpublishing.com
www.lidpublishing.com

A member of:

BPR
Business Publishers Roundtable

www.businesspublishersroundtable.com

Printed by CPI Group (UK) Ltd, Croydon CR0 4YY
ISBN: 978-1-911498-61-2

Cover and page design: Caroline Li & Matthew Renaudin

VISIONARIES
HUAWEI STORIES

TIAN TAO
YIN ZHIFENG

LONDON   NEW YORK   SHANGHAI
MADRID   BARCELONA   BOGOTA
MEXICO CITY   MONTERREY   BUENOS AIRES

Contents

The Bitter Cold of Winter Gives a Warm Fragrance to Plum Blossoms in Spring

Preface

By Sabrina Meng

In the past, we would
improve only after
we were aware of
our weaknesses.
We would take up
our responsibilities,
and stumble our way
forward into the light.
Today, we have a plan,
and act accordingly.

Ten years ago, Huawei's finance staff were criticized non-stop. They were criticized by our CEO Mr Ren Zhengfei, by business departments, by customers, and by employees. We were like a headless chicken, running around aimlessly and constantly weighed down by our work.

Today, 10 years later, we are still criticized. But the criticism is different now. Criticisms of finance are no longer about blame or complaining. The criticisms we receive these days express expectation, tolerance, patience, drive, and encouragement. We are like a tiny sapling yearning to grow. We are working hard and constantly improving.

In the past, we would improve only after we were aware of our weaknesses. We would take up our responsibilities, and stumble our way forward into the light. Today, we have a plan, and act accordingly. We remain dedicated to our beliefs, and work hard to create value. To borrow a metaphor from a well-known poem in China, "The strong pass of the enemy is like a wall of iron, yet with firm strides, we are conquering its summit." I am very grateful to Mr Tian Tao for bringing all of these many memories together into a single book. We've had good times, bad times, tough times, sad times... so many memories and emotions. Those memories and sentiments now accompany us as we look ahead, wings extended, aiming to fly higher.

I am confident that colleagues who have participated in the work depicted in this book will shed sentimental tears as they read it. I am even more confident that colleagues who work with us in the future will find enormous inspiration in these pages.

Opening Boundaries in Work

Projects are at the core of the company's business operations. Only by properly managing every project can an enterprise maintain robust operations. We assign a project financial controller (PFC) to support every contract. They assist sales managers in analyzing customer transaction habits, help delivery managers carry out careful site management, and support accounting teams to ensure our accounting is accurate. They engage proactively with contracts and projects and accompany delivery engineers to project sites and account managers during negotiations. Their hard work is apparent everywhere. They are doggedly persistent, and have an infectious sort of dedication and passion for their work.

One project CFO braved the scorching sun to reach a base station 120km into the desert. He conducted monthly audits on payments, and implemented road repair plans to clear the way for base station construction. He improved through practice, and practiced through improvement, and was ultimately able to reduce the road repair costs of the project by US$3.5 million. Another staff member travelled to a valley 2,000 meters deep to speak with site engineers and contractors about road conditions and the environment around the base station. He then formulated a delivery cost reduction plan for the valley base station. Even though the project only involved 10 base stations, the PFCs were as dedicated as ever, and won the strong, positive recognition of business teams.

In 2016, the exchange rate in a country in which we operate began to experience major fluctuations. Its economic prospects began to look very uncertain. The country's PFCs stepped up to the plate. They proactively engaged with the frontlines, engaged with customers, and played an enabling role, rather than just a supporting one. Before contract negotiations, they collected information and carefully estimated the potential foreign exchange losses for the entire period of contract execution. During contract negotiations, they participated in person to discuss terms relating to how the losses from foreign exchange could be shared. Even when negotiations became deadlocked, they remained positive and polite, and fulfilled their due diligence in protecting the interests of the company. After contract signing, they never let their guard down even for a moment. They remained deeply engaged in projects, tracked the progress of the company's delivery plans and the customer's payment plans, and proactively coordinated progress on both sides. Their aim was always to minimize the gap between cash outflow and inflow.

As the finance team, we have to be sure that we are living up to the accountabilities of our role. Opportunity management is not in our job descriptions, but is an optional bonus task and is how we create added value.

Our goal is to be the best finance practitioners in the ICT industry.

Opening the Boundaries of Management

In 2007, management of internal controls was kicked off as a project of the Integrated Financial Services (IFS) transformation program, starting the journey of Huawei's financial transformation. Rome wasn't built in a day and now, after 10 years of work, awareness of internal controls, internal control systems, and internal control capabilities are built into every business activity. Internal controls can be found wherever we do business, forming a global internal control management system founded upon process accountabilities and organizational responsibilities. This system is providing unique value in the company's operations management activities.

In the early days of promoting internal controls, finance was viewed as being in opposition to the business side of our operations. The goal of internal controls seemed to be to hinder the rapid handling of business. Amidst the confusion, we gradually found our positioning, and proposed the goal of demonstrating the value of internal controls by improving operating results. With this objective in mind, we softened our approach and broke the work down into smaller parts. We went to each regional office and each department, explaining to them what internal controls were about and determining the goals of their internal control work. Once we had goals, we made commitments. Once we made commitments, we had to live up to them.

The internal control team at one of our offices rolled out a system of automated acceptance, billing, and application of accounts receivable. This shortened billing time from 80 minutes down to 10 minutes, and the incidence of invoice refusals by customers dropped by 98%. From the perspective of internal controls, following processes made our work clearer and more standardized. From a financial perspective, revenues and expenses were accurately recognized, and customer payments could be more quickly collected.

Another office has a team that likewise focused on addressing the pain points in their business operations. Their primary focus was to connect up Huawei and customer systems where purchase order information could be found. Once the project was implemented, the current year discrepancy in accounts receivable was reduced by US$32 million, with a reduction of US$11 million in losses caused by goods rejected by customers.

These are all examples of how internal controls can imperceptibly bring about tangible business benefits, and gradually gain recognition and acceptance from the business side. When an enormous and complex machine kicks into action, internal controls act as the lubricant as well as the brakes. When we improve operations and optimize work, internal controls are the lubricant. When we are ensuring there are checks and balances and that data is transparent, internal controls are the brakes. Controls are not just about 'stopping', 'blocking', or 'safeguarding'. Controls must always revolve around the goal of *increasing our harvests and making our business environment more fertile.*

Opening the Boundaries of Control

Twenty years ago, Mr Ren Zhengfei proposed that the company should be guided by business and monitored by finance. We have gradually moved from a lack of understanding to a better understanding, and from non-acceptance to complete identification with this direction given by Mr Ren Zhengfei. Slowly but surely, we have built up our expertise in this direction. Our goal is not just to have profitable income and healthy cash flow. More important is that operating results are sustainable.

We began the internal control transformation in 2007, and now have a system of 'Four Threes' that we use to manage financial risk. In this design, the 'Four Threes' in risk management are: three types of risk, three financial risk control centres, three lines of defense, and three levels of review.

We divide the potential risks faced in business operations into three categories: strategic risk, operational risk, and financial risk. We then clarify and confirm the specific risks in each category, and ensure the person accountable for each specific risk carries out routine risk management work by identifying, assessing, addressing, responding to, monitoring, and reporting issues. The aim is to minimize the possibility of systemic risk.

The company's financial risk control centres in London, Tokyo, and New York carry out independent assessments from a professional perspective on financial architecture, financial strategies, operational activities, regulation, and stress tests. They act as the 'blue team' in finance, and conduct proactive review in key financial fields. They challenge the authority of the 'red team' and bring new perspectives to the table. The aim is to stem systemic risk and critical risk in finance.

We have three lines of defense built into our business processes, before, during, and after various activities. The first line of defense is business managers. They naturally assume process accountabilities and management responsibilities for their work. The second line of defense is the internal control and inspection team. They bring different methods and perspectives, and support business managers to effectively assume process accountabilities. The third line of defense is the audit team. They establish deterrence through irregular audits across all levels and domains.

The three levels of review are a system in which our books reflect the realities of our business and where all accounts match up. It is established by independent CFOs and centrally-managed accounting and treasury departments. At every level of management, we have established a financial organization, from the project level to the national level, and from support functions to business groups. Behind every manager there is almost always a full-time CFO supporting their work. The second layer of review is achieved through the process of accounting. The accounting team steps into the business. They ensure that the business data that flows into the accounting process meets the standard requirements for processes and permissions. They ensure that every item on the books has a tangible traceable source in business, achieving consistency between accounts and business realities. The third level of review is performed by the treasury team. They complete all of the bank account reconciliation work across the globe every single day, ensuring that every movement of funds has its source in the company's accounts, and making sure that all accounts match up properly.

The aim of controls is not control for its own sake. Rather, it is to establish systematic assurances through reasonable delegation and effective exercise of authority. By controlling 'surfaces', we ensure the enterprise is able to sustain its robust operations. By controlling 'lines', we ensure that critical risks and systemic risks are always controlled to minimal levels, and that no risks occur that the enterprise would have difficulty handling. By controlling 'points', we help management teams mature through self-reflection and self-improvement.

Teams on the ground are delegated command authority, and are willing to proactively exercise their authority. Organizations that assume global management responsibilities have oversight authority at back offices, and properly delegate authority with effective controls in place. This is the ideal we have in our minds when seeking to build our system of controls.

Opening the Boundaries of Our Organization

Within a dissipative structure, an organization must bravely stretch out and actively absorb new energy in order to obtain new drive for ongoing growth.

Over the past two years, finance has been hard at work opening the boundaries of the organization and absorbing fresh energy, welcoming in outstanding talent from around the world. In November 2014, for the first time, the finance team held a finance-focused job fair in the UK. This was the first step taken to expand our pool of overseas talent. Huawei's finance team now has several hundred students from Oxford, Cambridge, Harvard, Yale, and other renowned universities, who are becoming a new driving force for us. In them, we see a powerful desire to change the world, to realize the value of the organization, and to drive personal growth. They are passionate, driven, methodical, patient, and very strong learners. They have a very open mindset and are knowledgeable. They give us great hope for the future as we look ahead to them gaining a steady footing and accelerating their pace of development. We hope that these young people will be able to rapidly develop and grow, and bloom in all their brilliance.

At the same time, we establish organizations and build up our expertise in areas where talented people are abundant.

The tax planning team and intercompany transaction team have already relocated to London. A portion of functions relating to foreign exchange and cash asset management have also moved to London. We have found that top financial experts are more easily acquired in Europe and the US. These talented people are highly skilled and experienced, are very influential in the industry, and have excellent information channels. By joining our company, they help to bring our own expertise to the next level, and open doors of thought that were previously inaccessible to us.

To have the opportunity to work alongside such inspiring top experts is the best non-monetary incentive imaginable for our young people who are so eager to grow.

Opening the Boundaries of Thought

Of all the boundaries out there, the hardest to break down are the intangible boundaries of thought. If we want to keep up with this ever-changing era in which we live, we have to shake free from the shackles of our own thinking and actively experiment with new methods and new tools. We have to break down boundaries in how we do our work and bring with us new perspectives and new stances. We are very lucky to be able to grow with a leading ICT enterprise. We are lucky to be a team that has opportunities, capabilities, and an awareness of the need to utilize advanced tools.

In the field of accounting, we are actively trialing automation and smart functionality, handing over the accounting work in standard scenarios to machines. Each year we handle over 1.2 million employee expense reimbursement tickets alone. Employees are able to handle expense reimbursements online, and the system directly generates vouchers based on predetermined accounting rules, which then drive the generation of bank payment orders. Payment orders are then sent to banks around the world in less than two minutes. Computers also handle the daily bank account reconciliation work, and automatically check for variances between each movement of funds and accounting records. Suspect transactions are flagged for manual review.

Our global program of connected asset management using Radio Frequency Identification (RFID) is now implemented across 140,000 fixed assets at 2,382 sites in 52 countries. RFID tags are attached to fixed assets. Every five minutes, they automatically report a location signal, and once per day we update the usage load state of the fixed assets. After we deployed RFID, the time required to count fixed assets around the world was reduced from months down to only a few minutes. For each year's asset counting work and asset inspections, we saved upwards of 9,000 person-days of work. The timely update and sharing of information about asset location and idle assets really got us on track in our asset management.

We have seen impressive creativity from the four big data projects involved in cash planning. We have now officially launched big data projects for operating cash flow forecasting and cash flow forecasting by currency. Based on big data modeling, computers carry out ten thousand calculations and model iterations. Operating cash flow is now forecasted on a 12-month rolling basis.

Compared with historical data, the smallest variance is only US$8 million. Our company conducts business in 170 countries and regions, and has an annual revenue of about US$80 billion and an annual cash settlement volume of approximately US$400 billion. So a variance of US$8 million in rolling forecasts of cash flows is an ideal result.

The 'Videowall' information hub for tax accounting is soon to be deployed in London. Basic information, tax payment compliance data, trade routes, rolling forecasts, and other information about the company's subsidiaries from all around the world will be centrally displayed on this screen. This will help us to build a highly efficient organization for global mobile operations that is available, ready, and capable to act at any time when we face uncertainties in financial results and tax practices.

Opening the Boundaries of Capabilities

There are countless stories to be told of the journeys of growth and development in the finance team. There are tales of perseverance, dedication, and a spirit of craftsmanship and excellence, supporting the organization as it pushes ahead in business.

The implementation of the project for consistency of inventory accounts and goods (CIAG) has made site inventories visible, countable, and manageable for the first time in the company's 30-year history. CIAG for site inventories rose from 76% in 2014 to 98.62% in 2016. Off-book materials in global central warehouses worth US$88 million were re-used, and we dealt with US$75 million worth of overdue inventory. We achieved a major improvement to the age structure of inventories at central warehouses and sites. Each of these tangible and real achievements has proven that we are a team that does what it says it will do. In 2014, experts from delivery, supply, and finance departments formed a joint working group and set the goal of achieving CIAG worldwide within three years. They were true to their word, and achieved that goal. Today, CIAG worldwide is a reality.

We now have a system globally that works 24/7 for our accounting. We have made full use of the advantages of time differences at Shared Service Centers (SSCs). Working on the same data platform and using the same accounting close rules and same system logic, the SSCs work together to handle accounting close work, which has significantly shortened the actual days required for close. The system works around the clock to automatically deploy accounting close data on a rolling basis. Over 170 systems are seamlessly connected, with 40 million lines of data processed every hour. As we like to say, "The sun never sets on the SSCs," as they provide financial data at the fastest possible speed to more than 130 offices and business entities. On the fifth day of every month, the company's more than 200 subsidiaries around the world are all able to produce financial reports in compliance with local, Chinese, and international accounting principles.

Traditional finance services have long since fallen to the wayside as the primary target in our work.

Finance is now a part of every aspect of company business, from contract estimation to project payment collection, from product planning to market analysis, from business travel applications to expense reimbursement, from asset management to inventory management, from sales financing negotiations to implementation of financing plans, from tax planning to pricing. The finance team has developed from a state of 'utter backwardness' to being 'somewhat backward', and on to the present day, where we can confidently say that we are 'somewhat advanced'. As an old Chinese poem goes, "I see the petals falling out in the courtyard, and gaze out at the swirling clouds in the sky." There is so much more I could say about our work.

By compiling this book, Tian Tao has pulled together stories from a decade of development in finance work at Huawei. This book records memories, emotions, and hard work. You will read stories, and also come to understand some of the lessons we have learned along the way. The content is a testament to our achievements, and also encouragement to continue on our journey.

When you are traveling upriver, if you stop rowing you will go backwards. We have to work harder, be more dedicated, and more open. The flame of youth can ignite an entire life without regrets.

Youthful Aspirations Blooming in Africa

By Sui Long

My first job after graduating in 2012 was at Huawei.

As a rookie in the company's regional finance management department, I was prepared to head overseas on my very first day with the company. I was eager to accomplish big things in the world so that I would have something to remember on the long journey that is life. I wanted to make the most of my youth.

Shortly after I passed my interview with the CFO of the Southern Africa Region, I found myself on a plane to the Maya–Maya International Airport in Brazzaville, the capital of the Republic of the Congo, on 26 July 2013. When we safely landed, thunderous applause broke out in the plane cabin because everyone was so relieved to have landed without incident. This marked the start of my adventure in Africa.

Assuming Heavy Responsibilities as a Rookie

Before I came to the Republic of the Congo Office, Liang, CFO of the Congo Office, told me I would be simultaneously managing the finances of projects, the country office, and the local subsidiary. After hearing this, I thought to myself that Africa really could provide a broad platform for me to unleash and realize my full potential. A great weight of responsibility was resting on my shoulders, even though I didn't have much experience. I could not wait to get down to work. On my first day, I saw the title on my business card: CFO, Republic of the Congo, Huawei Technologies. I couldn't help but feel a great sense of pride and responsibility. I told myself, "I may not be a qualified CFO yet, but I will bridge the gap in the shortest time possible and provide strong support for the business operations of the Republic of the Congo Office."

There were, of course, many difficulties to address after coming to a new country, but I was ready. All of my colleagues were very patient, walking me through various issues in the office in great detail. I managed to get started in my new role very quickly.

However, working in three positions at the same time demanded a lot of effort and attention, and sometimes I felt the need for extra hands to help me complete my work.

The company's HQ was at that time rolling out Project Financial Management (PFM), a new initiative in which I was also involved. I had to improve our financial processes, and also introduce the company's new requirements for project financial management to business departments at regular meetings.

I also had to deal with all sorts of financial issues in the Republic of the Congo Office, from checking the reimbursement of business trip expenses by employees and reviewing payments made to suppliers, to the office's Key Performance Indicator (KPI) forecasts and how key projects were doing. While spending most of my time handling financial issues, I used any spare time I could find to improve myself and learn about finance management in subsidiaries. I wanted to bridge gaps in my capabilities to support operational compliance in the subsidiary.

In this way, I learned while working and worked while learning. There was a long period of time during which I started work almost immediately after getting up in the morning and only stopped when I went to bed at night. I had to input more time and effort than my more experienced and skilled colleagues. But all hard work pays off eventually. After one year, I managed to support the normal business operations of the Republic of the Congo Office, and concluded a key financing project. I also won a 'New Business Expert' title, granted by the Southern African Region.

My first year in Africa was busy and fulfilling. This period was also the first time for me to celebrate the Chinese Spring Festival in another country. After I got up on the morning of the Spring Festival, I called my parents in northeast China. Hearing their familiar voices and sensing their love for me, a sense of loneliness crept up within me. I hung up the phone after speaking only a few words to them. I didn't watch the CCTV Spring Festival Gala either, because I believed it would bring me to tears. That night at a dinner with colleagues, I purposely drank a lot of wine.

By the time I woke up, it was the afternoon of the first day of the Chinese lunar calendar. I then decided to take my laptop to the office and work.

"You Want to Freeze Our Money? No Way!"

One day in 2014, our local cashier called me from the bank, sounding very anxious. He said to me: "The treasury has frozen our bank account." I was shocked. We had never received any official notice about this.

After several failed attempts, I managed to meet the individual working for the treasury who was responsible for the issue, and I demanded an explanation. Seeing that I wasn't going anywhere, he took a notice out from his drawer announcing the freezing of Huawei's bank account. He then said: "The tax bureau demanded that Huawei's account be frozen. We didn't get a chance yet to send this to you."

The Republic of the Congo is located in central Africa. Huawei established a local subsidiary in the country in 2008, and by 2013 our annual revenue there was into the tens of millions of US dollars. Since the establishment of the subsidiary, the local tax bureau had imposed several fines on Huawei, citing reasons that in our view were sometimes not justified by law. The fines by that point totaled several million US dollars. For these tax cases, we had paid deposits according to local laws and were defending ourselves against the tax bureau. According to local law, before a conclusion was reached on the tax cases, the tax bureau had no right to freeze our bank account.

There was no time to lose. I immediately called the company's tax consultant and explained the situation to him. We agreed that our top priority was to ensure the security of the money while working to unfreeze our bank account as soon as possible. This would ensure the smooth, continued operations of the subsidiary. I immediately started work with our tax manager to prepare four official letters. One was addressed to the treasury, explaining the status of the tax cases and asking them not to transfer our money. Another was addressed to the tax bureau, asking that our bank account be unfrozen.

We received a response from the treasury the day after we sent the letter, and they promised us they would not transfer the money. This meant that our money was safe for the time being. However, the letter to the tax bureau went unanswered, and we could not reach the head of the tax bureau by phone. The subsidiary had several upcoming payments to make, including employee salaries.

So they wanted to freeze our money? My answer was: "No way!" I decided to visit the tax bureau in person.

It was raining heavily that morning. I took a thick local tax book with me that could substantiate our position in law, and headed to the tax bureau with our tax manager. After hearing that we were from Huawei, the receptionist told us that the head of the tax bureau was in a meeting, and was unavailable. We were also not allowed to wait in their office, so we stayed at the gate. Two guards soon after asked us to move to the yard of the tax bureau, urging us to leave. We refused. The rain was pouring down by then, so we opened an umbrella and continued to wait in the yard. After waiting from 9am in the morning to 8pm at night, we finally caught a glimpse of the head of the tax bureau. We thought we had finally found the person who could solve our problem. But before I was able to say anything, his bodyguard 'escorted' us from the yard.

We were unable to defend our cases. At our wits' end, we had to escalate the issue and seek support. With support from the company, we figured out the departmental structure and functions of the local tax bureau. We got ourselves up to speed with the rules for joint operations between the tax bureau and the treasury. Thanks to our professional defense, we finally were able to get our bank account unfrozen. This also gave us new insight into how we could close the tax cases.

"Huawei Good! Regen Good!"

After the bank account crisis was over, several rounds of negotiation about our tax cases began to draw the attention of the local government. The finance ministry assigned a chief judge to oversee the hearing for Huawei's tax cases. The Congo Office also set up a dedicated team for tax case closure, and we called for experts from the region and HQ to support us.

In the early stages of discussion, the tax case trial team, headed by the chief judge, adopted a tough stance. Our communications with them often did not go well. They did not understand Huawei's business scenarios very well, and would often raise a number of questions about a very simple business scenario. We had to answer every question in great detail. For example, it took us a lot of time to explain terms like 'base station', 'spare part', and 'managed services' to the trial team. Even after these explanations were provided, it was still common to see perplexed looks on their faces.

After several months, no substantial progress had been made on the tax cases. I was very worried. We could not continue this way. Something had to change. We wondered if there was something we could do to help the trial team to understand Huawei's business. Oral and written descriptions are often boring and abstract. Because of this, they would often be ineffectual, as had been proven by their failure to work so far. I wondered if they could see Huawei's business scenarios and how Huawei operated with their own eyes; then perhaps it would be easier for them to understand us. My idea was backed by leaders of the Congo Office.

In July 2015, the trial team visited Huawei's campus in Bantian, Shenzhen. After spending several days there, they gained a clearer understanding of Huawei. After the visit, the chief judge changed the tough stance he had previously been unmoved by. In fact, he even got a little excited. He held my hand and told me: "Huawei good! Regen (my English name) good!"

After returning to the Republic of the Congo, the trial team became more familiar with our business scenarios. The expert team at HQ also provided us with generous support. The trial process was becoming smoother, and a breakthrough was made one month later. Six of our nine tax cases in the Republic of the Congo were closed, and the tax risk exposure was reduced from several million US dollars to US$150,000.

When we received the closure letter, I was so happy that I shouted out, "Great! We finally did it!" I rushed over to Li, Director of the Republic of the Congo Office, and told him the news. "Well done! Let's celebrate with some drinks tonight!" He gave me a thumbs up. When toasting with colleagues about this success, I could not help but recall everything we had been through over the prior two years: the nights reviewing every detail of the cases; the debates and discussions; and the talks with customers. It had been an extremely tough process, but in the end it was all worth it.

At the end of 2015, I was transferred to South Africa, to work on project finance at the regional office. There, I was mainly responsible for managing the standard actions for project estimation, budgeting, accounting, and final accounting, as well as associated processes and internal controls. Such a shift in responsibilities meant a big change in thinking for me. My perspective of projects changed, and I had a new understanding of my job as a project financial controller.

In the past, I had never quite understood what 'standard actions' really meant. After a period of study, I realized that all KPI management aims to help field offices identify problematic projects and issues. As CFOs working in field offices, we need to pay more attention to projects that have issues, identify the root causes, develop feasible solutions, and ultimately resolve the issues. In my first six months in South Africa, I studied everything I could get my hands on regarding the region's business operations, and did everything I could to ensure projects operated smoothly.

We could hear explosions, which seemed to be getting closer and closer. We were very nervous.

The Third Type of Relationship Developed by Working Outside China

During my first three years with Huawei, in addition to gaining work and life experience, I met a fantastic group of friends. When it comes to friends, it is often said that there are two types of relationships that are most precious: relationships between classmates and relationships between fellow soldiers. For those who work outside their home countries, I think there is another type of relationship that is also very precious: the relationship between colleagues. I found this to be particularly true in the Republic of the Congo, where expats live and work together. The relationships between colleagues are very sincere and caring. Such relationships are developed over time and after sticking together through thick and thin.

I still vividly remember something that happened one morning at the end of 2014. Everyone was busy working in the office as usual. Then, suddenly, a colleague who sat beside the window saw that everyone on the street was running out of town. Armored cars filled with soldiers were heading towards the Presidential Palace. Something was afoot.

It quickly became apparent that internal turmoil was brewing. We could hear explosions, which seemed to be getting closer and closer. We were very nervous. It was the first time we had ever experienced something like this. We all gathered in a small office that was far away from the windows to avoid stray bullets and wait for the conflict to end. We comforted one another, and some colleagues even shared some jokes to ease the tense atmosphere.

In the afternoon, there were more explosions. The violence outside showed no sign of stopping. After extensive discussions and preparations, the local office decided to transfer us to a safer location outside town. At first, a stifling silence permeated the car, leaving everyone feeling depressed. Then a sudden burst of gunfire frightened our logistics manager. Seeing this, a product manager beside him started telling us his corny jokes to calm us down. We found that our nerves were eased a bit

33

after laughing at the jokes. Someone said, "We are experiencing a war. We are now brothers and sisters. We've been through a life-threatening situation together."

In addition to these dangerous moments, we also took care of one another at work and in life. In the early hours one morning, I came down with a high fever, and had no medicine. I asked in our WeChat discussion group if anybody had medicine to treat a fever. Around 10 minutes later, our product manager Lin knocked on my door, panting. He handed me the medicine he had just picked up from the drug store. The next morning, he even sent me some breakfast.

Such experiences and moments have built deep relationships between us, bringing us together like the roots of an old tree.

Tying Knots to Make a Net

Many people have asked me whether my life in Africa is bitter. I often respond with another question: "Can you tell me what is sweet?" When the first group of colleagues who had worked in Africa shared their experiences with me, I think what they experienced could be called bitter. The company has been stepping up efforts to improve the living and working environment in regions where employees may experience hardship. I wouldn't call our life outside China bitter anymore.

When I first arrived in the Republic of the Congo, malaria was a serious problem. We would often stay up late at night when project schedules were tight, and that was when we were most likely to contract the disease. During the year when I was focusing on dealing with tax cases, I came down with malaria three times, and my colleagues would call me a workaholic. There was a difficult recovery period after catching the disease. However, after recovering and seeing that my work had solved real problems and helped support our business, I felt a great sense of satisfaction and it all felt worthwhile.

Life can be both bitter and sweet. I saw African children who had no shoes but nonetheless wore the most beautiful smiles you could ever imagine. I also saw billionaires who squandered money every day but whined about their boring life. What is sweet? Maybe to understand and cherish 'sweet', we first need to know what 'bitter' is. I'd like to thank the company for giving me the opportunity to experience these things. I would also like to thank my younger self for working hard and enduring the bitter things I've been through. If I had the chance to make the choice again, I would still choose to come to Africa, because working in Africa is not a bitter experience.

Our CEO Mr Ren Zhengfei once said that we need to tie knots with the threads we own, and by tying knots, we can make nets, with which we can catch fish. After working in Africa for so long, I have been able to tie many meaningful knots, and I look forward to tying many more.

Sui Long

12 Years Without a Single Error

By Mary Ma

In 1999, I earned my master's degree and joined Huawei, working in the Global Payment Center. No payment can be made at Huawei until the Global Payment Center gives the go-ahead. I am the final check before Huawei sends instructions to the bank to make a payment from our accounts.

When I first started, of course, I was the new girl in the office. Now, nearly 20 years later, I am a mentor for the fresh-faced youngsters, who call me 'big sister'. Every day, I deal with payments ranging from just a few yuan to hundreds of millions. My records show that I have processed 1,036,000 payments, and my run of zero errors is now 12 years long.

In 2016, I was honoured to be voted a 'Payment Craftsman' in the first selection of this award. People often ask me how I have managed to go so long without any errors. After all, no one is perfect! Actually, my 12-year run started with two errors.

The Two Errors that Bought Me a 12-year Perfect Run

Many people wonder how it is that I have managed to avoid making a single mistake for 12 years straight. Is it because I'm just a stickler for detail?

Actually, it's got nothing to do with my character. When I joined the company, I was not a detail-oriented person at all. I certainly made mistakes back then, two of which were quite serious.

My first job was as a cashier. I was ambitious and confident, and I wasn't pleased about being put in this position. I thought to myself at the time: I have a master's degree; this job is beneath me. However, I made two critical errors within just one month. It was a real blow to my confidence. These two errors had a significant impact on my career, and even today, after so many years, I can still remember every detail of what happened.

We were dealing with two suppliers with very similar names – just one or two letters different. When I was checking the documents, I didn't notice the difference, and combined the two payments to the two companies into one. It was a sum of about US$1,000.

A few days later, I was reviewing a payment to another supplier. I should have deducted an advance payment we had already made, but I didn't do so, and instead authorized the full payment, this time for about US$2,000.

When the department did its monthly review of bank statements, these two critical errors were detected. When my manager sat me down and very seriously explained them to me, I was stunned. But she did not blame me. Instead, she patiently helped me analyse the cause of my mistakes. I realized that it was my attitude: I was overconfident and under-skilled, and I had not given my work the attention it deserved. I was trying to dash through the work as quickly as I could. I had not seen the job for what it was: the first step on a long road. And as a result, I had made some easily avoidable mistakes. I felt very upset with myself. "I can't even get this right! What am I thinking? I should first get the basics done right!" I am still very grateful for how my manager handled the situation back then. She gave me another chance, and together we contacted the suppliers to correct the errors.

From that day on, I have always reminded myself that it doesn't matter how many times you fall. What matters is that you get back up again.

Every time I made a payment, I first circled the key information on the payment voucher. After I filled out the bank notes, I checked each item, one by one. I reminded myself that this was not just arithmetic homework. Money matters! So, I had to stay focused and coolheaded: more haste, less speed. Whenever I had time, I would sort out all the documents needed for payment: contracts, customs declaration forms, receipt statements, foreign exchange applications... That way I didn't get flustered when the payments started rolling in.

I spent 10 years working as a payment accountant, churning through payment data day-in, day-out. Then, in 2011, I was promoted to a job with more responsibility – payment approver.

Payment approvers perform the final checks before company money is paid out. Everything the company buys has to be signed off by me, from the food in the canteens and goldfish in the ornamental ponds to the company shuttle buses, and million-dollar payments to suppliers and customers.

Any mistake I make could cause the company's cash to go bowling out the door, so the responsibility is a heavy one. I had plenty of experience by this time, but still I was haunted by the memory of those two mistakes I made when I first joined the company. I asked myself whether I was truly ready for this new job.

Over 40 Seals and 3,000 Documents per Day

But the pressure only hardened my resolve. If the company put its trust in me, then I would become the best!

One of the key responsibilities of a payment approver is to endorse documents with company seals. The company seals are very powerful instruments. They are like the signature of an ancient commander, powerful enough to send thousands of men marching back and forth. The slightest error in the use of company seals can cause incalculable losses.

The first time I opened the two boxes and was faced with the more than 40 different company seals used for financial documents, I almost fainted. Dozens of seals of different colours, materials, and shapes. There was horn, bronze, plastic, red rubber, black ink. Some were photosensitive or self-inking seals. Some of them were round, some oval, and others square. Some had covers, some did not.

How on earth was I going to use them? I had no idea at all. These seals had previously been looked after by various finance managers, but after I became the financial approver, they handed all the seals over to me. I myself would be the sole manager of the seals. But there was no one who knew how every one of them was supposed to be used. There is an old saying in China that goes: "If you don't have a teacher, then you *are* the teacher."

I searched online for answers and found that the use of seals was not as simple as met the eye. Different stamps require different types of ink: traditional ink pad, photosensitive ink, special ink for self-inking stamps, you name it. Each kind of stamp needs to be inked up in different ways, using an ink pad, refilling from the top, or turning the stamp upside down. Online there were stern warnings: don't mix up your inks or you can destroy your seal!

After a few days' research, I took some scrap paper and tried them all out. They should have been easy to use at that point. However, when I tried using them, I found it was hard to create the perfect impression. If you didn't get it just right, the image would be smeared or too light. The desk was too hard and the seal slipped. But if I put a pad under the paper, the surface would be too soft and the impression would be distorted. I spent a whole night on it, trying all possible positions: I sat, I stood, I bent. I tried to apply the seal with my left hand, right hand, and both hands. I put a magazine or a calendar under the paper... Finally, I found the perfect way: putting the document to be endorsed on a mouse pad, and then applying the seal. Later, I even codified a standard procedure for myself: hold the seal in your right hand; line it up; press down with the left hand on the right hand; silently count to three.

During the course of my work, I also found that each document has its own rules for sealing, so there was a lot to learn. For example, there are six major things you want to avoid when endorsing bank acceptance bills: Don't let the stamp ride on any lines on the bill. Don't cover over other seals or signatures. Don't tilt the seal. Don't blur the seal. Don't use the wrong seal. Don't forget to stamp across the perforations. When I had finally internalized all of these rules, with my standard procedure, I was finally able to produce perfect impressions.

I started to love the beautiful patterns of a well-applied stamp. To me, they feel more refreshing than sunset in the mountains, a breeze on a lake, or birdsong in a wood. It's no exaggeration to say that when I wield my stamps, my mind's eye sees the happy smiles of people around the world as they use their phones.

Using the company stamps is a technical skill, but more than that, it is a test of willpower and of speed. Before host-to-host payment was massively deployed to give direct connectivity between Huawei and our banks, I would have to endorse 2,000 to 3,000 separate pieces of paper a day during peak periods. Just using the more conservative number, 2,000, means applying a seal once every 15 seconds.

When I was faced with a huge stack of documents, I took a deep breath. Then, I started by sorting them into order of importance and urgency. After checking the recipient bank information, and all of the internal approvals, I started the actual stamping. No payment can be made if there's no money in the bank account, so the first items I handled were those relating to internal fund management: transfers between accounts, wealth management products, and fixed term deposit accounts. Then I could start on the regular payments. I left the bank acceptance bills till last, because they have strict requirements, and there were always lots of them. Every time I endorsed a document, I double checked it afterwards to make certain there had been no error.

During some busy periods, I might work from morning till night. When I finally get home for dinner at eight or nine in the evening, my hands will often be so worn out that I can barely feed myself. At those moments, I always plan to start a regime of regular push-ups for more strength, but somehow it never quite happens!

Looking at the Bigger Picture Saves Three Million Dollars

The reason that I am able to work this way has nothing to do with my natural inclinations. I can tell you that anyone can be more accurate than a machine, so long as you have a sense of responsibility and solid expertise, and follow processes closely.

First is expertise: you need to know the accounting procedures inside and out, otherwise you will never be able to spot problems. Second is process compliance: when you are an approver, you have to know whether a transaction will be profitable or loss-making; whether it is compliant with company policies; whether it has been properly approved. You need to know all these details, and there is no room for error. Huawei operates in over 100 countries and has over 1,000 bank accounts worldwide. Each day, the company makes tens of thousands of payments, totaling hundreds of millions of US dollars. And every single payment has to be approved by a financial approver. Protecting Huawei's money takes strict compliance with the processes, a strong business acumen, and high-quality output.

I like to learn new things, so I always take the time to learn the ins and outs of entire processes. I often spend time checking things that others might think are completely pointless. I never take things at face value. Deep-diving into the documents can help me spot problems more quickly. For example, what bank is a payee using? Usually, you would assume that it is the bank named in our accounting system. But assumptions are at the root of many an error. One Huawei employee had the People's Bank of China – China's central bank – down as his personal account bank in our accounting system. Fairly obviously, that's not possible!

I like to check things, even if they are (strictly speaking) not my responsibility. In theory, as long as I can see that the process has been followed, then I should sign off on a payment. But as I am the final check of payments, stricter requirements are imposed on my experience and acumen. As far as I'm concerned, responsibilities cannot be confined to a specific role. So, as well as checking process compliance, I will check whether the payment is normal and reasonable, just to make sure we're not about to walk compliantly onto a landmine.

This habit not only ensures that I make no mistakes, but also helps me prevent any major losses being incurred by the company as a result.

One day in 2013, I was informed by a subsidiary that it needed to pay a large amount of money to a supplier. The subsidiary said that it was an urgent request, as the local bank was going to close soon. All of the approval documentation was in order, but I knew all the subsidiaries that made large supplier payments, and this subsidiary was not on the list. So, I went back and checked the whole process, looking at the original documents. I knew there must be something wrong. It turned out that the invoice being paid was issued two years ago. The payment was close to three million US dollars. In fact, the supplier and Huawei were still in the process of settling a dispute, so the payment had to be frozen.

It is simple enough to check for problems, but my instinct that allows me to spot those problems has developed over more than a decade of experience. Without it, I would never have achieved my long, error-free run.

Dedication Makes the Ordinary Sublime

Over the years at Huawei, I have handled a million payments safely and swiftly. These payments underpin the successful rollout of mobile towers and optical fibres. I have made a tiny contribution to the Huawei vision of 'Building a Better Connected World'. This gives me a sense of pride in my work.

I have to say that my record of 12 years without an error is not really my own record at all. It is the product of a good team, and of good work done improving and smoothing company processes.

I have been here in the finance department for a long time and I have seen plenty of changes over the past 20 years. In 1999, the Global Payment Center had only a dozen or so staff members. We mainly worked on the payments of the Group. At first, payments required a cashier to fill out a form by hand based on the original copy of the accounting voucher, which then had to be stamped by the payment approver before the payment could be made. That meant that at the end of each month and each year, we were overwhelmed by documentation. We would have four or five boxes with a stack of documents 40 or 50cm high. I often felt like I was drowning in a sea of documents. However, this was my work.

My impatient nature was gradually tempered and, in the end, I learned to keep a calm state of mind.

In 2013, the company started to introduce a host-to-host payment system giving direct connectivity between Huawei and our banks, using SWIFT codes. In 2016, our smart payment system went live. Now, this system directly sends payment orders to our banks, ending the need for so much paperwork. It has made our payments much more efficient and accurate.

The award I received was called 'Payment Craftsman', but I have never felt that I deserve that title. It was just my job to check every bit of payment data, and process compliance. I never did anything special. All of my colleagues in the Global Payment Center do exactly the same thing. Every one of us is committed to doing the best job we can, from little details like filling in transaction notes and remarks on invoices, to major projects like bringing new systems online and finding ways to improve our processes. All of us are constantly thinking, discussing, and sharing ways of improving our work, to make the payment process as good as it can possibly be.

Every single employee is like a vector: we all have a magnitude and a direction, and we are much stronger when we work in the same direction. It is the craftsmanship of the entire team that really makes our payments secure and our processes fast.

The function that we perform is quite an ordinary one, I suppose, but if we can stay committed, just as committed after 12 years as on the very first day, then I think we can hold our heads up and say that we have done our part for this company, and done our parts as professionals. That's something we can all feel good about.

The spirit of craftsmanship means that our time here has meant something.

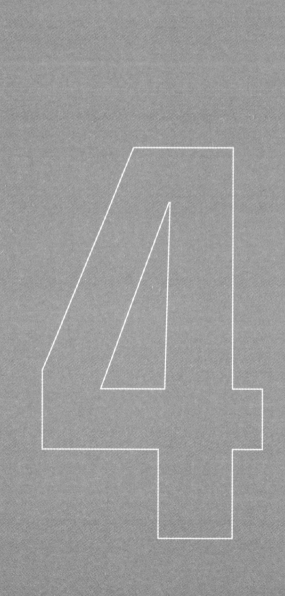

From Radar to Sixth Sense

By Evan Bai

"The more rapidly we develop, the higher risks we will encounter. In addition, we face great risks in our operations. In the 170-plus countries and regions where we operate, we face all kinds of risks, including wars, diseases, and currency-related issues... We do not hold back because of risks, nor do we ignore risks in order to progress."

When I look back at how the Huawei Financial Risk Control Center (FRCC) has grown over the last four years, what I remember most clearly is something our CEO Ren Zhengfei said when he visited us during a trip to London: "Finance needs to be solid, and the business team needs to be bold." He then asked us, "How can the finance team carry out solid, accurate, and low-risk financial operations for the company on a global scale? How can we ensure internal and external compliance, generate more revenue, and protect our future success?"

Risk Is Everywhere

During a meeting with former British Prime Minister David Cameron in London in September 2012, Mr Ren Zhengfei announced that over the next five years, Huawei's investment and spending in the UK would total GBP1.3 billion, and would generate 700 new jobs in the UK. This would represent an important step towards free trade between the UK and China. Huawei's decision to establish the FRCC in London was a result of this meeting.

However, the company's vigilance against financial risks goes back to the 2008 global financial crisis. I still remember the second half of 2007, when the company announced that we needed to bring the business side and the finance side closer together. We were going to create mixed teams that understood both business and finance. At that time, I was working in the Corporate Development Department, and we had just finished the negotiations to establish a joint venture with Symantec – a software security company in the US. Less than a month after that project was finished, I was told that I was being transferred to finance to manage the Sales

Financing and Treasury Management Department. Soon afterwards, I was given a lesson in finance that I would never forget: the catastrophic financial crisis that swept across the globe in 2008.

Telecom was a fast-growing industry at that time. In many countries, a variety of licenses were fetching sky-high prices at auctions. Telecom operators and investors were all looking for ways to utilize financial leverage so that they could do more with less investment. This led to exceptionally strong demands from operators for new equipment, and for financing deals, but at the same time they were particularly prudent with their cash outflows, including equipment payments. Prices were negotiated hard. As a result, Huawei was growing fast in this period, but along the way we had built up a great deal of financial risk.

The first issue was an unbalanced cash flow. Cash is the blood in a company's veins, but Huawei neglected the importance of cash flow indicators. During those years, Huawei would usually have a negative cash flow throughout the first 11 months of every year. Finally, in the last month of the year, sometimes in the last two weeks, the payments would come in and Huawei's cash flow would increase dramatically. It was very impressive to see. All of the hard work we had done over the year was suddenly turned into a fountain of money that streamed in from dozens of different countries all over the world. You could see eyes light up at the sight of our newly-bulging bank accounts. But that kind of uneven cash flow meant liquidity risks, and we were forced to issue the company's first ever warnings about operating cash flow at the end of 2007, and had to do so again at the end of 2008.

The second issue was our high debt ratio. We were growing fast, but many of our operating assets had long payback periods. That meant that in the short-term Huawei needed financing from the banks for liquidity needs. Ultimately, our debt ratio (nearly reaching 70%) became a major concern. At that time, our debts were mainly fixed-term obligations to banks and suppliers. Today, we have a much stronger cash flow, and a considerable proportion of our debt is in bonus accrual.

Back then, our local offices focused on profit margins, and our ability to manage cash flow was relatively weak. Profits are good headline material, but cash flow is the nitty gritty of our business. Our days sales outstanding (DSO) was often as long as 140 days, which meant our capital turnover was very slow. We had to borrow a lot to keep the company ticking over. One notoriously difficult customer in India used to stretch out its payment time to over 1,000 days. Once when our CFO, Liang Hua, returned from another round of squeezing payments from that company, he decided that we must better manage our operating assets. Again, it seemed that sometimes finance only wins respect when something goes wrong. When the company finally put its mind to solving the problem, we managed to shorten our DSO to less than 80 days. We have also improved our ability to get good contract terms and to use strong currencies. Today, over 85% of our contracts are denominated in major trade currencies. Huawei's Integrated Financial Services transformation project, which is improving finance across the whole company, has helped improve the situation significantly.

Another thing which Mr Ren Zhengfei often talks about is the problem of foreign exchange management: "The company lost US$1 billion because of poor forex management." Juggling multiple currencies is always highly risky. You'll recall the collapse of Barings Bank and the bankruptcy of China Aviation Oil (Singapore) following hedging losses of US$550 million, as well as Société Générale's US$7 billion and JP Morgan Chase's US$2 billion in hedging losses. The financial and foreign exchange markets are fast-moving and can create huge risks. Early on, Huawei did not strictly manage and plan the currencies we should have used for our contracts, so we signed a large number of contracts denominated in the customer's local currency. However, we lacked the ability to manage forex forward transactions. After the global financial crisis began in 2008, emerging markets and non-USD currencies all fell drastically. Huawei reported US$830 million in exchange losses in 2008 alone. That is why Mr Ren Zhengfei often reminds us of this error, and tells us to learn from the experience of the industry. He says that we must harvest a large amount of grain, but also that it must be good quality grain. Today, Huawei's revenue has grown by several times compared to what it was back then. Along the way we have experienced a series of other crises, but our figures show significantly less volatility in our forex gains and losses.

Going International

With our increasingly rapid overseas expansion, Huawei urgently needed more overseas financing. Before 2007, 90% of Huawei's financing came from domestic sources. But at the end of 2011, after four years of careful planning, this had been completely reversed: over 80% of our financing came from outside of China. This means lower financing costs and gains in foreign exchange. This in turn helps us meet the company demand for liquidity. More importantly, it helps Huawei link into international capital markets, which means we are better protected against a financial shock in any single economy.

Many moments from the Treasury Management Department are still vivid in my mind. I remember the first time our cash holdings topped US$10 billion, and US$20 billion. I remember the first time we obtained a US$1 billion financing deal from an international syndicate of banks. I remember the first time we issued private bonds overseas, and our first issuance of public bonds overseas. I remember our first international multi-currency cash pool, first forex transaction worth over US$10 billion, first significant forex forward transaction, and first major use of workarounds for trapped cash... Today, Huawei manages a portfolio consisting of more than 130 currencies, with transactions that reach trillions of US dollars. We have capital ticking over in more than 170 countries and regions across the world. When you see all of that, you can understand what it means when they say "money never sleeps." All of these breakthroughs were possible thanks to the skills

and experience we developed in the aftermath of the great financial crises. We learned to handle risks in the midst of risks!

Because of the growing size of our capital assets and our
increasingly complex capital operations, Huawei has to think
hard about how to secure our global operations. In order to manage risks and prevent future crises, Huawei made the decision to
roll out a global treasury structure and establish international
treasury centres in key locations where we could access the strategic resources we need.

Europe is an important market for Huawei, and also an
important centre of international financial institutions. Wei Guo
and I led a team to European countries including the United
Kingdom, Ireland, Luxembourg, and the Netherlands in 2012
to scout potential locations for our new International Treasury
Center. The Netherlands has a number of well-known banks and
financial institutions, including ABN AMRO and ING, a large
number of multinational companies, and an attractive tax regime.

Evan Bai with the giants of the International
Treasury Center in the Netherlands

It also offers lower costs and is closer to our local offices than the international financial centre of London. Eventually, we decided to build one international treasury centre in Amsterdam. It would initially serve the four regions of West Europe, Northeast Europe, Central Asia, and Russia, gradually expanding to cover the entire EMEA (Europe, the Middle East, and Africa) region. Another treasury centre is located in Hong Kong, where it can interface with the large number of international financial institutions there, and manage capital operations in the Asia-Pacific Region.

Zeroing in on London

The meeting between Mr Ren Zhengfei and Prime Minister Cameron in 2012 eventually led to Huawei's decision to build the FRCC in the UK. The company assigned me to take charge. I joked that it was probably because I had a reputation as a risk-taker at the Treasury Management Department – now the company wanted me to be a poacher-turned-gamekeeper. I had many ideas for financial trade that were denied by management. This experience helped me understand Huawei's deep commitment to sticking to our own industry, and not getting caught up in risky investments elsewhere. A key idea in Huawei's approach to risk management is focus: focus on the customer, and focus on our core business.

We had many questions when we were setting up the FRCC. Huawei is not a financial institution, so why did we need a centre for financial risk control? How could this centre effectively manage our financial operations? What value would this centre bring to the company?

We got advice from HSBC and Standard Chartered Bank, had long discussions with British Petroleum, Vodafone, and major international companies, and talked to the big four accounting firms, trying to figure out exactly what role and responsibilities the FRCC should have. As the months passed, our understanding gradually became clearer. The banks had been improving their risk control mechanisms since 2008 to combat an unending series of regional financial crises: the never-ending European debt crisis, currency slumps in emerging markets, Russia's national risk, the oil slump, and so on. Huawei's business growth is exceptionally rapid and complex. Huawei operates in more than 170 countries and regions and manages more than 145 currencies. This is more than most banks. It is a web of financial complexity. But this high-speed growth contains the seeds of enormous risks. We need to invest human resources and money into powerful risk controls to counterbalance our incredible expansion. That will make us more resilient against future uncertainties and ensure that we can continue to grow in the long term.

Evan Bai

The FRCC focuses on making sound business decisions following an excellent business process. The FRCC is there to challenge us to improve our financial skills on an ongoing basis. In the 2008 subprime mortgage crisis, the rating agencies followed their process to the letter when rating mortgage assets. Financial institutions also followed their process when they securitized the assets and used them for investment and trading. However, the ratings were wrong, and greed caused many banks to hold too many interrelated assets, which eventually blew up in their faces.

The lesson is that we can only properly control risks when we have good processes and make good decisions. One important area of focus is building the skills needed to monitor financial risks, and to review key policies, rules, and business. This will ensure that we have the ability to see and forestall the build up of systemic risks. That way, when a 'black swan' event occurs, we will be ready. The role of the FRCC is to give an independent voice, challenge business owners, help improve business, ensure process compliance and existence of economic substance, and be a key part of our solid, low-risk financial operations.

Putting Down Roots in London

The City of London, the 'Square Mile' surrounding the Bank of England, is one of the world's most important financial centres. The Bank of England was the world's first central bank, known as the 'Old Lady of Threadneedle Street'. It has witnessed many ups and downs in the financial industry during its three centuries of operations. George Soros famously "broke the Bank of England" in 1992, when he forced a run on the pound. But during the 2008 crisis, the Bank of England was a pillar of stability. Over this same period, the City of London weathered these same storms and crises.

The City of London is currently the world's largest market for currency and derivatives trading, bond trading, and cross-border loan transactions. It hosts more than 600 financial institutions, including the headquarters or regional headquarters of globally recognized banks such as HSBC, Standard Chartered, Royal Bank of Scotland, Deutsche Bank, and many others. The headquarters of PwC, Ernst & Young, and other accounting firms are also situated in London, along with world-famous law firms, and the International Accounting Standards Board (IASB). The City of London also offers a high-quality and fair legal system and regulatory environment, a finance talent pool unlike anywhere else, and an open and inclusive cultural environment. All of these were exactly what Huawei needed to achieve operational excellence in finance.

Therefore, the City of London was the ideal location for Huawei to build the FRCC, as we wanted our strategic centre in a location with abundant strategic resources.

In early 2013, we started recruiting in London. We very quickly found that we were looking at a pool of highly professional finance talent, who were able to make long-term commitments, and were very competitive in terms of salary. As an international financial centre which has grown steadily over decades, London has nearly a million financial professionals in the city. In addition, London hosts the headquarters or regional headquarters of many financial institutions, so difficult projects from many regions are submitted to the headquarters in London for final decision-making. This means that practitioners in London grow fast.

Bringing in experts created tangible value in our work. For example, Luis is a Spanish banker who used to work on counterparty risk in a Spanish bank. He sensed the subprime mortgage crisis three months before the collapse of Lehman Brothers. Therefore, he promptly warned the bank about the high risk of bond trading with Lehman Brothers, and recommended that it sell off its large holdings of Lehman Brothers' subprime bonds, helping the bank to avoid significant losses. After Luis joined the FRCC, we asked him to set up early-warning systems for the financial market. In this way, we were able to use the webs of capital to identify the risks of economic crises, major currency fluctuations, counterparty banks, and customer credit.

Time is money, and being one step ahead or behind the market can make all the difference, so timely acquisition and processing of information are critical. For this, we engaged and worked closely with the risk control departments of Citigroup, HSBC, and Standard Chartered Group. Our positive relationships with their top management also helped us acquire information on national sovereignty risks early on, giving us a bigger window within which to respond.

We also learned lessons from our failures during the early days of the FRCC. One deeply regrettable experience was that at the beginning of 2013, a country in the Mediterranean region was hit by the European debt crisis, and its financial situation was worrisome. At that time, the FRCC had only just started operations. We discovered the crisis and gave an early warning. However, we hesitated a little before taking action, due to a lack of experience. We had just finished our internal discussions and decided to take action when the government announced a rescue plan for its banks. It put a freeze on capital outflows, and forced the owners of accounts in troubled banks to become shareholders in those banks. In the process, Huawei suffered losses of about US$600,000. However, the FRCC learned an important lesson, and later we were sure to liaise closely with local offices and HQ to take immediate action when necessary. We were thus able to avoid significant losses during events such as the Greek debt crisis, the Ukrainian crisis, and the slump of the Russian rupee.

A good example of our ability to avoid significant losses came at the end of 2013, when a crisis broke out in another country. Before the crisis began, there had been unusual volatility in the financial market. We gained a great deal of information from the banks we were working with, and we acted at the same time as them to protect our interests. The local Huawei office also took quick action to help us protect Huawei's funds and assets in the country. Beyond the initial crisis in this country, we realized that the crisis could easily spread to a neighbouring country. We warned management of the risk to this neighbouring country, and, soon after, the currency of that country began to dramatically devaluate. Many foreign investors in the country suffered massive losses as their local contracts were denominated in the local currency. But we were able to control our losses, as we had anticipated the risks and taken the appropriate action.

At the end of 2013, Huawei's third ICT finance forum was held in London, and Huawei CFO Sabrina Meng officially announced the opening of the Huawei FRCC there. The FRCC would be responsible for managing risks across major areas of our financial operations, including accounting, liquidity management, foreign exchange risk management, credit management, and global financial compliance. By assessing and controlling financial risks, the FRCC would help Huawei roll out coordinated and low-risk financial activities around the world so that we could continue to provide high-quality services to our customers. The FRCC was then formally in operation, with three teams separately working on treasury, accounting, and tax risks. The FRCC does not replace the risk monitoring function of process owners, nor does it intervene directly in processes – it neither reviews nor approves any part of the treasury, accounting, or tax processes. Instead, it offers an independent review of the major policies and programs used in those processes, and presents its conclusions to the CFO and process owners for reference.

A party at the FRCC's new offices in the City of London

Exploration, Innovation, Convergence

We have a lot of experience monitoring risks in the treasury function, but effective risk controls in tax and accounting were a whole new challenge for us. We could only keep on trying new things and running exercises, and ultimately this system of trial and error would help us find suitable approaches.

Different countries have different tax policies, so the FRCC tax team needs to identify and quantify tax risks within the context of each country's compliance rules. It then determines the total level of risk, challenges the existing tax management practices, and offers recommendations for improvement. In the third quarter of 2014, Vodafone UK's tax director, Richard Needs, joined Huawei and led his team to develop a tax risk map, which did exactly that.

Since the beginning of 2013, the FRCC team has been bolstered by the arrival of experts from major banks, the big four accounting firms, and other multinational companies. We aimed to build an elite team, and it has now stabilized at about 30 members. The Tax Management Department has moved its global tax planning and transfer pricing functions, and some of its direct tax and indirect tax functions to London. This decision was made in light of the huge pool of talent available in the city. The Accounting Policy Center has also settled in London. Treasury has long seen London as a first-choice location, and has moved its foreign exchange, asset management, and international treasury functions there. It was estimated that by the end of 2017, there would be nearly 300 employees in London (130 in the tax COE, 70 in the treasury COE, plus accounting, sales financing, etc.). This wealth of talent will greatly enhance Huawei's capacity to perform all of its global operations.

Entrants in a Huawei-sponsored finance contest for British university students

The FRCC also transferred many expert staff to other departments to strengthen the business. The humorous and quick-witted Ben Binnington, who served as the director of accounting policies at Barclays Bank for 10 years, helped clear many doubts on financial accounting policies. The delightful accounting specialist David, who worked at HP for many years, was sent to support another department. And Luis Martinez also ended up being transferred to the treasury department to work in areas like proactive risk management.

A Sixth Sense for Risk

The FRCC has now been operating for three years, and every branch of the finance department has set up a centre of expertise (COE) within the FRCC, with all branches seeing improvements in their ability to control risks as a result. In 2015, the Huawei Group Finance department asked the FRCC to work specifically as a 'blue team': This meant that it was tasked with finding problems with our current systems. The team should develop completely separate risk management approaches that are well coordinated with those of COEs. Therefore, the function of the FRCC has shifted from being a standard risk 'radar' to building up a 'sixth sense' for financial risks. It carries out independent reviews and challenges our finance departments, and offers early warnings to the business side, the CFO, and the company leadership. This ensures that the company as a whole is more capable of recognizing and managing financial risks. The most important feature of the FRCC in this 'blue team' role is its independence.

This is actually a very difficult procedure. It is our duty to identify, anticipate, mitigate, resolve, and transfer risks. And our goal is to make it all look effortless: preventing every risk before it emerges. Peter O'Donoghue, who was a Deloitte partner for 23 years, currently manages the FRCC's work product. He said that our ultimate objective is to make the FRCC redundant. This can happen only when all of the specialist insights the FRCC provides have been incorporated into the company's day-to-day financial operations, placing us at the very forefront of the industry.

Following the success of the FRCC in London, the company has now asked us to set up the Macro Economy Analysis Center in New York. Its job will be to create a macroeconomic dashboard that enables Huawei to take the pulse of the world economy. We have also established the Project Operating Risk Control Center in Tokyo to learn from the professionalism of Japanese companies and to accelerate the development of project management skills within Huawei.

We still have a long way to go, but we are always moving forward. We explore, try new things, stumble, and pick ourselves up. We hope to construct an 'iron shield' that will repel financial risks, from global macro-events down to projects. We hope to be the defenders of Huawei's future.

A consortium of banks that works with us in Hong Kong

The Long Road to Profitable Business

By Lin Wei

A few days ago, I was cleaning out my bookshelf at home when a photo dropped to the floor. I picked it up. It was a group photo taken at Bai Cao Garden, an apartment complex provided by Huawei for its new staff. We took that photo when I had just joined Huawei, in early 2006. Looking at the photo, I couldn't help thinking nothing beats you harder than time! It's been 10 years, long enough to accumulate a few good stories...

"You Must Make Payments On Time!"

When I started at Huawei, my first job was in the Latin American regional office as an accounts receivable accountant. My responsibilities were to keep the books, reconcile our accounts with customers', make sure the accounts of both sides matched, resolve any inconsistencies, and apply accounts receivable.

Back then, the company was introducing a new Enterprise Resource Planning (ERP) system. As part of that process, I was sent to work in Venezuela for a time. Soon afterwards, we started building an accounting shared services centre in Argentina, and I ended up being part of that project, too. Soon I was flying back and forth so often my head was spinning, but eventually, the company decided to keep me in Venezuela. I started working on accounts receivable there, and soon took over budgeting, project finance, and some other duties.

The general manager of the Venezuela Office told me: "Your number one priority is to make payments on time!" The Venezuela Office was growing rapidly and had many turnkey projects with many contractors involved. If anything went wrong with payments, the contractors would be very unhappy, and projects would probably be delayed. We also had payments to make for utility bills. If the payments were late, the power and water might be cut off to the office or the apartments where our staff were accommodated. Colleagues would be left without anything to eat or a place to sleep! We couldn't afford that. So, I kept reminding myself: payments, payments, payments. If a payment was delayed for some reason, or any other problem occurred, I had to find out what had gone wrong. Was it the documentation sent in by our local office? A problem during the review process? Or an issue with bookkeeping? Every time there was a problem, we would find a way to fix it and improve the process so that it didn't happen again. Luckily, we had no major problems during the year or more that I did that job.

In 2007, I was promoted to the position of finance manager of the Venezuela Office. Back then, finance people actually spent most of their time doing the accounts: keeping the books, reconciling our accounts, issuing invoices, making payments, and preparing monthly consolidated reports. Our financial systems were underdeveloped, and Huawei's ERP system still didn't properly extend to our region, so we weren't able to drill down into the detailed financial data, let alone do monthly operational analyses or rolling forecasts, which are pretty standard procedures today. As I said, the main job for a finance manager at that time was basic accounting tasks like making and collecting payments, reconciling accounts for intercompany transactions, and producing timely reports. The foreign exchange controls in Venezuela were another challenge. Our major concern at that time was filling out the proper paperwork for the National Commission for Administration of Foreign Currency (CADIVI) so that we could transfer money out of the country in US dollars.

The finance team in Venezuela celebrating the Christmas holiday, 2007

Winning the contracts was only the first step. Our people now began to worry: how were we going to deliver two huge projects while keeping our customers satisfied, our quality high, and our costs well-controlled?

Finance Staff: Hidden Away at the Back

In early 2008, when I was back in China on holiday, I received a call from Fang Weiyi, then president of the Finance Management Department, who asked me to come and see him in Shenzhen.

He was direct: "I want you to work in the India Office. Can you convince your family?"

I thought for a moment, then gave my reply: "No problem."

So, I went to India as assistant director of the local finance department.

India was a huge market and 2008 was a big year for Huawei. Shortly after my arrival, the company won a major turnkey project which involved the construction of more than 10,000 base stations. Soon afterwards, along came another project of about the same size, which meant the office now had over 20,000 mobile base stations to build.

Winning the contracts was only the first step. Our people now began to worry: how were we going to deliver two huge projects while keeping our customers satisfied, our quality high, and our costs well-controlled? Finance was still very much a backend function at that time. We were not involved when the sales teams were bidding for projects, so we weren't able to give realistic cost estimates, particularly project delivery costs. That meant we didn't have a good cost control solution.

I still remember those projects as if they happened yesterday, because they were such incredibly hard work. I can see those budget meetings now: teams from different product lines were pounding the table and yelling at each other.

"There is no way we can shave any more off our costs!"

"Well, it's exactly the same for us!"

Each night, a dozen or so people from the wireless, network, and energy product lines sat together and tried to hammer out the most cost-effective bill of quantities (BOQ). We argued and worked into the small hours in order to work out the best solution.

Wang Xudong, who was in charge of project delivery for the entire Asia-Pacific region, was the project director for these mega-projects. I often used to run into him in the smoking room. He would finish his cigarette and give his face a brisk rub, then dive back in to continue with the BOQ. During the day, we watched the international copper and iron exchanges to see whether the prices might drop. And then the product lines met in the evenings, usually through the entire night, to negotiate a workable plan. When we had the best solution we could find, we would take it to the customer to try to get their sign-off on any changes to the specifications.

After many rounds of meetings, we eventually came up with a final BOQ for the projects. To be honest, we had no idea at all how much money the projects were going to make, or lose. We had decided to take them on because we thought they were important for Huawei to expand into the Indian market.

Project Estimation: An Experiment in India

We did in fact lose money on both of the projects. But that taught us an extremely valuable lesson. We realized that finance needed to move out of the backend, and into the frontlines. Up to that point, the only job we did in most projects was accounting. When sales teams bid for a project, they didn't involve finance, so they didn't know if it was going to make money or not. So, I started to think: could we produce project estimates in advance?

I went to talk to Dr He, who was vice president in charge of products, and he agreed with me right away. So, we began to pilot full cost estimation for projects in India. I led the finance team through the change into this new mode of work. Project estimation would be an integral part of all processes, so we had to work out a feasible methodology for setting up cost baselines and working out the full estimate. We decided to learn by doing, and began estimating costs for each project as it came up, exploring the right method along the way.

After we had produced a few project estimates, colleagues started to accept and use our figures. For the first time, finance people were invited to the meetings when the sales team prepared for bidding. The local office asked us to confirm the cost with Huawei's product pricing centre, and only then would we send the estimates to the general manager for review.

Once we had successfully produced accurate estimates for a number of projects, this new procedure became routine for the India Office.

Then there was a debate on whether cost estimation should be done for all company projects. When I flew to Shenzhen once, Fang Weiyi asked me: "Is project estimation worth doing? Is the finance department the right department to do it?" This question took me aback for a moment, but after a second of thought, I was sure: "Yes! It is a good technique for the whole company!"

After completing several projects in India, I had a basic understanding of how finance should work, how we could engage with our sales teams, and how finance could help make our projects profitable. Near the end of my time in India, I helped in a training workshop to teach Huawei CFOs, and my story was included in the training materials.

The finance team in India, September 2011

The Key to the Problems in Brazil

In September 2011, I was appointed CFO of the company's South Latin America region. Brazil was my major concern. Huawei had been in Brazil since 1998 and had never turned a profit in 13 years. Before I set off to take up my new post, my boss grabbed me by the shoulder and gave me this instruction: "Make Brazil profitable!"

The Brazilian market is very complex. You can see it in the Brazilian tax system, which includes three separate layers of taxes: federal, state, and municipal. There are also additional taxes on industrial products (known as IPI) and all kinds of restrictions on what can be sold to whom. Brazil manages this complex system by tracking invoices, and the whole process is highly digitized. Every invoice must be recorded in the computers of the national tax bureau.

In this complex environment, Huawei experienced a period of 'wild growth' when it first entered the Brazilian market. We grew very fast, but we didn't have the proper backend systems, and we made many errors and incurred a lot of unnecessary costs. We were very imprecise in the way we worked. If the customer asked for 10 base stations, we would often deliver equipment and materials for 12 stations; once we'd got all these materials, we would then go and build 10 stations – after all, so long as we built the 10 required, the customer wasn't complaining! But all this imprecision resulted in a lot of excess inventory and complete chaos in our books. The warehouse in particular was a comedy of errors. When we had to clear it out to move to new premises, we found 164 containers' worth of old stock that shouldn't have been there – we didn't know for which projects or contracts they had been shipped. We had to ship the whole lot back to China.

When I arrived in my new office in Brazil, I was actually very anxious. Colleagues say two things about Brazil: one, that it's beautiful but treacherous, and two, it's all about the nightlife. Brazil is one of those places that looks incredible from the outside, but doing business there is actually incredibly hard. And when Huawei staff talk about the nightlife, they mean staying up till two or three in the morning for meetings because of the time difference with HQ in China. I knew the Brazilian market was tough, so I spent two months figuring out why Brazil was like that and how we could improve the situation. The South Latin America regional management team met many times, trying to find the key that would shift us into the black in Brazil. And eventually, we identified a path that seemed promising. We decided we needed to build up our competitive strengths in integrated, end-to-end operations. That meant we would streamline end-to-end processes and become more skilled at integrated planning. Could we link up every purchase order with a clearly identified customer need? Could we accurately and efficiently handle more than 100,000 purchase orders, along with the hundreds of thousands of invoices? Could we increase the level of detail and granularity in our project financial management?

Better Processes with ERP and IFS

My title was still CFO, but my responsibilities had changed significantly. Before I went to Brazil, I had focused more on accounting and finance and seen myself as a partner of business teams. Now I had to change. A new transformation team had been set up, led by the regional president himself. I was asked to be the project team leader, and then became the director of the Process Quality and Operations Committee for South Latin America. I would no longer just take care of finance. Legal affairs and IT departments reported to me as well. My role was now similar to a COO or CIO, as I helped the regional president manage internal operations for the entire organization.

The major reason we had failed to make the Brazil Office profitable for so many years was that our financial processes were a mess. To streamline these processes, I chaired a meeting each Friday morning with all the departments involved to discuss how to transform the finance operations of the entire Brazil Office. We needed improvement across the board, from basic purchase order management and invoicing to process capacity building. I posted up a diagram of the whole Opportunity to Cash process on the wall of my office, and I used to study it every day, thinking about how we could make the process flow better.

The Brazil Office issued over 100,000 invoices each year. During our busiest time, we had more than 200 people responsible for invoicing. Inevitably there were a lot of errors. Invoice errors could cause significant trouble: customers could reject the invoices, or we might have to pay more taxes. Efficient, accurate invoicing was an immediate concern for us.

In April 2011, we launched an ERP system in Brazil but it got stalled at the user acceptance test phase. Not a single invoice had been issued in three months. When I arrived in Brazil, customer complaints were flooding in. Since shipments can only be released together with their invoices, no invoices meant no shipments. Our work had come to a complete standstill.

But we pressed on, and the ERP system did ultimately bring significant improvements. Because of the complexity of Brazil's tax system, we often misclassified our invoices into the wrong tax category. We launched a project to ensure that ERP was the only source of correct tax rates applied to invoices. When product managers were creating BOQs, they would use the tax rates in the ERP system. We also helped customers prepare orders. They would confirm the orders and scan the key information into ERP. The system would provide the correct tax rates automatically based on the key information. Automation brought consistency, and finally we were able to apply consistent tax rates and issue correct invoices. Pretty soon we were able to cut the number of people working on invoicing from more than 200 down to 60.

As the processes started to run more smoothly, and our supply capacity grew, customer trust began to climb. A customer who had complained several times actually came and told me: "Terry, we don't need to worry about working with Huawei anymore!"

These days customers don't rush to place orders. They first make sure their base station construction plans are complete and settled before submitting the order. We have put in place strict rules for the internal processes as well. If we haven't received a complete, formal purchase order, with all materials specified, we will not start manufacturing. If the purchase order for software or services doesn't match the hardware order, we won't deliver the hardware. Now that we were getting our order processing right, we were giving customers correct invoices, and we became stronger at project delivery. It used to take two months for us to deliver materials and equipment to the site after the customer sent us an order. Now it takes much less time, often as little as two weeks. As we continued to improve, Brazilian customers placed more trust in us – it became a virtuous cycle.

Making Difficult Decisions

Although our business in Brazil was getting better, we were still recording losses. Finally, in 2013, the Finance Committee rejected our annual budget for the next year. I spent 90 minutes on the phone trying to argue our case. I was almost in tears, because if the company did not approve our budget, we could not plan for the year. Any time we didn't collect the receivables we expected, we would be left without any money to pay our bills. The stress was crushing. But I thought about why I came to Brazil in the first place and I realized that I had to tough it out.

The Brazil management team was determined to make Huawei Brazil profitable in 2013. When I flew to China in mid-2013, the chairman of the Finance Committee, Guo Ping, came in person to listen to my report.

When I returned to Brazil, I told the team the news that we would not take on any new managed services or microwave transmission projects; our existing projects in these two areas must not be expanded. Huawei Brazil just didn't have the exper-tise or the resources necessary to support these areas. They were both very expensive areas to work in, and Huawei Brazil didn't have the cash to burn or the ability to deliver these projects cost-effectively, so every managed services and microwave project we did was losing money. We had to make the business decision to get out of those markets, and only return when we had the expertise to do them well.

In 2013, Mr Ren Zhengfei came to visit us in Brazil. His encouraging words greatly boosted team morale. That year, the Brazil Office became profitable for the first time in its history. Continuing the upward momentum, 2014 and 2015 also saw increasing profits. I was proud to see that Huawei Brazil was becoming an industry leader for fast, cost-effective delivery.

The time I spent in Brazil was one of my most precious experiences. I went to Brazil as the CFO for the South Latin American region. As a CFO, you need to know the technical side: accounting skills, a proper understanding of the business, and a good command of business skills. You also need to know the art of the CFO: communicating with internal and external stakeholders, handling and controlling risks. A CFO has three major functions – supporting business growth, managing finances, and controlling risks. I often tell people around me that my career at Huawei has neatly covered every part of the definition of a CFO.

Celebrating Christmas with colleagues in Brazil, 2014

Conclusion

In 2015, I was reassigned again, this time to London. Every day I take the Tube to and from work, threading through the bright financial centre and the skyscrapers of the city, and I think of how far I've come. My ten-plus years in the finance department seem to have flown past. There have been happy moments and there have been tough moments, but it's definitely been a learning experience.

Happiness comes from a life packed with memories!

Lin Wei in Argentina, 2015

Leaving No Stone Unturned

By Mi Jiansi

"Cleaving to the mountain never letting go; roots sunk deeply in jagged stone" are the first two lines of *Bamboo and Stone*, a famous poem by the Chinese painter and poet Zheng Xie. I particularly like these two lines. The 'jagged stone' tells us that the bamboo is growing in barren land, but it still looks for a chance to grow. It takes root, sprouts, and eventually towers above the other bamboo plants.

Laying Down Roots Overseas

After graduating from the China University of Political Science and Law in 2006, I joined Huawei's Intellectual Property Rights Department. After a little time there, I was transferred to the Legal Affairs Department, where I was part of the dispute resolution team. One day in 2009, Song Liuping, the Chief Legal Officer of the company, asked me whether I wanted to work in a country I'll call 'Y'.

Y was recognized as one of the most challenging countries for our company. The country's natural environment was harsh, and doing business there was complex. We seemed to get embroiled in a lot of disputes, so it was a tough posting for anyone. I had been to Y once before, so I knew how far behind China it was in terms of infrastructure and economic development. However, I had also seen that there was a lot of room for the legal team there to make a real difference. So it didn't take me long to decide to take the assignment. I was sent to Y and assumed the position of Deputy Director of the local Legal Affairs Department. I didn't have too much trouble adjusting to the physical conditions, as I myself had grown up in a poor village in China.

However, the work didn't go smoothly. It felt like I was running underwater. The residents of Y were welcoming and friendly, and loved to say yes. Whenever you asked them to do something, the answer was, "No problem!" But it often turned out to be a big problem. To give a simple example, when you asked a taxi driver on the phone whether he could get to the courthouse in five minutes, the taxi driver would always say yes. But the journey might end up taking half an hour. We encountered similar problems in our work. Huawei requires its employees to finish whatever they take on. You have to be able to get things done. But the local lawyers who worked with us had a very different ethic. They would always eagerly agree to our requests, but often failed to deliver on their promises. I took a number of dressings down from my department head as a result of this.

Despite the difficulties, I still believed that Y was a place where legal affairs could really shine. The company faced many challenges there, which meant opportunities for us. Y might contain a lot of 'jagged stones', but I was determined to take root there and grow like bamboo.

Fighting a Debt Collection Battle

In 2009, X Group signed a contract with Huawei for 2G equipment and services worth US$156 million. But it still hadn't made the final payment of US$128 million in 2012. The parent company owed Huawei US$118 million for equipment, and two subsidiaries owed us US$10 million for services.

Our local office and headquarters had negotiated with X Group many times, but there seemed to be no way to collect this money without pursuing extraordinary measures. Huawei was preparing for the worst: making bad debt provisions. When the Huawei Finance Committee (FC) discussed how to collect the debt, Dr Song suggested that legal action would be effective, because the company we were trying to collect from was not lacking in funds. We could launch a court action against X Group. Taking a customer to court was always a last resort in a commercial dispute, but in the end the FC authorized the Corporate Legal Affairs Department to sue for the unpaid debts.

In July 2012, the Corporate Legal Affairs Department set up a project team with the local office. The core members of the team were G, the director of the local legal affairs department in country Y, R, and me. We led the preparations to use legal means to collect this debt of more than US$100 million. In order to be more efficient, we reported directly to Dr Song, so that we didn't get bogged down with other intermediaries.

Country Y has a relatively impartial legal system, but it is not very efficient. According to a government report, civil trials take an average of 10 years to resolve. Arbitration, on the other hand, is relatively efficient: it usually takes two to four years. In addition, our customer was very well established in country Y, and had strong influence in local politics, business, and the legal system.

G had a very good understanding of the law and of the business environment in country Y. He suggested a multi-pronged strategy to compel the customer to fulfill its contractual obligations. According to the law in country Y, if the customer couldn't repay its debts, Huawei could file litigation forcing it into bankruptcy. Therefore, we first filed two bankruptcy proceedings against X Group in the local court, demanding immediate payment for the debts owed to Huawei. If they didn't pay, the court would declare X Group bankrupt, and liquidate its assets to pay off the debts. As this was going on, our team also selected arbitrators, following the procedure in our contract, and launched three arbitration proceedings against X Group, requiring it to pay its debts to Huawei with interest. We simultaneously filed multiple lawsuits against X Group. It was all guns blazing to recover our more than US$100 million!

Unturning the Stones

After we launched the lawsuits, we quickly realized that our company was just one of many creditors trying to get money from X Group. This customer was involved in multiple lawsuits filed by several companies. In fact, X Group had so many debts that it had long since stopped worrying about them. X Group executives even sneered at our attempts to reach a peaceful resolution through other channels. "Haven't you filed lawsuits against us? We'll see you in court." This made me a little anxious, because the other side was trying to turn the matter into a war of attrition. If we really followed the full legal process of this country, we might get our money, but it would undoubtedly take at least five or six years.

More than six months after we filed our first lawsuit, we had been to court many times, but had not seen any progress whatsoever. Everyone was feeling the strain. I had to make regular reports to Dr Song and Cai, the general manager of the local office, and it was mortifying to have to report the same thing every time: "No progress." But they were very patient and encouraging, and continued to have faith in us and our ability to turn things around.

The team was feeling down. I used to chat with G, and one day he taught me an English saying: leave no stone unturned. I learned that this saying means to do everything that you can, but it seemed especially meaningful to me, because it transported me back to my childhood. Along with my friends, I used to go into the fields to catch little scorpions. The scorpions used to hide underneath stones, so just as in the saying, we had to turn over every little stone in order to dig them out. Seized by this thought, I got G and R to sit with me and went over the case once again: Had we turned over every stone we could in this case? Was there some detail that we had missed? Had we been too narrow in our focus?

The three of us started to devote most of our time to X Group. We watched the news and read the newspapers every day, and kept our ears open for every scrap of information about them. We found that as well as being a telecom operator, X Group also had oil and gas holdings. Now it just so happened that two of the country's leading oil firms were about to make an overseas acquisition of an oil field worth US$2.45 billion in a country I'll call 'M'. Several clues suggested to us that the oil field they were about to buy belonged to X Group.

This discovery was like spotting the light at the end of a very long tunnel. Now we had an angle. If we could demonstrate that the oil field belonged to X Group, then X Group definitely had money. If X Group had money but refused to pay its debts, then we could get an injunction from the court preventing the sale.

That might just give us the leverage we needed to turn the tables on X Group.

We began to look into the oil field in country M, but it was hard to get clear information about it. The data we collected in country Y was second-hand and scattered. It wouldn't stand up in court. For better evidence, we needed to turn over some stones on the ground in country M where it was all happening.

Before I set off on my trip, I reported to Cai. He clapped me on the shoulder, and said, "We are counting on you." In May 2013, I arrived in country M. The local Huawei office gave me a lot of help. They arranged a car, and took me to meet all the contacts who had any connection to the sale of the oil field: local lawyers, the head of the mining ministry, an advisor to the president, staff at the Chinese embassy... I followed leads and looked at papers. Sometimes I wasn't allowed to take photos, and had to copy down notes by hand. I turned over a lot of stones, found a lot of leads, and amassed an increasing compendium of evidence about X Group.

I made a second trip to country M in August that year. After two visits, we had a clear idea of the deal that was going down: the location of the oil field, the current market price, who the buyer was, what approvals they had to get, progress to date, and its connection with X Group. More importantly, we also had a complete chain of evidence. We went into our next court hearing brimming with confidence.

Piercing the Veil of a Front Company

In the first session of our suit against X Group held at the Supreme Court in country Y, we submitted a motion to freeze the assets of X Group, to prevent it from selling off any properties before paying Huawei. In the first half of the session, X Group's lawyer hardly seemed to be paying attention. He thought there was no chance the court would support us. But as we revealed more evidence collected in country M, the lawyer started to become more worried. The atmosphere in the courtroom changed, and the judge was clearly leaning towards our side after we presented the complete chain of evidence. At the end of the session, the court issued a ban on the sale of the oil field, and their lawyer rushed out of the room, sweating hard.

Our countless long nights at the office had paid off. We had made a major breakthrough. This turned the tide, and put X Group on the defensive. G, R, and I jumped and laughed like children on the steps of the court. People stared at us, but we didn't care.

We had interfered with a US$2.45 billion sale. Now X Group was feeling the pressure. They soon hired the country's top lawyer, who was also a major politician, and appealed the ruling.

X Group had a superstar lawyer. We had a good lawyer, but just from a local mid-sized law firm. It looked like a pretty uneven match. But we had our own ideas about how to pick a lawyer. The first lawyer we hired was well-known, but we quickly found that famous lawyers have to work on multiple cases simultaneously. They don't give their full attention to your case. We were worried when we started working with the new lawyer since he was not particularly well-known. But G said that he seemed very committed, and that reassured us. Events also proved that he was a bulldog, hungry like a wolf. He worked very hard for us, and he appreciated Huawei. We made a good match. During the case, he devoted himself to our case, and made many good suggestions.

X Group appealed on the grounds that the companies which were to sell the oil field were registered in Mauritius and the Virgin Islands. They were subsidiaries, or subsidiaries of subsidiaries. The transaction was to happen outside country Y, and denominated in US dollars, so the court of Y did not have jurisdiction, and Huawei had no reasonable claim or reason to interfere with this sale. We had anticipated these arguments and had already prepared well. I had worked out the complex relationships behind the ownership of the oil field, and R had converted all the information into one clear diagram.

In court, our lawyer presented R's diagram in an effort to illustrate the relationship between the companies. The company

that owned the oil field had only a few million dollars of registered capital, and yet after just a year of operation was about to
make a sale worth US$2.45 billion. This clearly showed that the
local holding company was a front, and that its actions were in
substance the actions of X Group. We argued that, this being the
case, X Group should pay Huawei before being allowed to sell its
oil field. We had pierced the veil of this front company, turned
over the right stone, and revealed the real owner of the oil field
lurking underneath: X Group. At 3pm on 20 December 2013, the
judge ruled that X Group must deliver to Huawei with a bank
guarantee on sight within seven days.

X Group decided that it was better to lose an arm and live
to fight another day. In order to proceed with the sale of their
oil field, X Group had no choice but to deliver to the court a
bank guarantee worth more than US$100 million, issued by
the London branch of the central bank of country Y. Once the
bank guarantee was issued, the bank would pay the money upon
the court's request, whether X Group agreed or not. The bank
guarantee was like a tonic. It was almost as if we could see more
than US$100 million waving to us...

However, our work was not yet done. Over a year or more of
back and forth, our team chased down every detail, and uncovered a number of opportunities to press our suit. In total, we
prepared and filed 15 lawsuits.

Difficult Negotiations

The bank guarantee was a turning point. "We've got them by
the neck now," we used to joke. And there was a sea change in X
Group's strategy: they became eager to negotiate with us. Huawei
agreed to talks as well, because we wanted to keep X Group as a
customer, so we hoped for an amicable resolution.

X Group now became the suitor: it proposed paying 50 cents on
the dollar, then 70 cents, then 90 cents. They pressed us for a resolution, and Dr Song came out in person to meet with them twice.

The issue came up for discussion at the FC meeting. Many people worried that if we didn't give X Group a discount, we might end up with nothing. However, Dr Song took the longer view. We should not be in a rush to accept what was on the table. "No discount," he said. "We see the legal process through to the end, no matter how they negotiate with us. Otherwise, we open ourselves up to more tricks and delays from X Group." From that point onwards, every time Cai received a call from X Group looking for a discount, he would stick to his guns: "Please discuss this with our Legal Affairs Department." He didn't allow them even a scintilla of hope.

At the same time, X Group made a number of overtures, threats, and blandishments to us. Private offers came to me and R: "You are still young, and we can help you if you want to have a successful career in this country. Let's discuss what you want." We just laughed. Our resolve never wavered for a moment.

G had to deal with more situations. He was threatened several times over the phone by lawyers and senior executives from X Group. One day after court, G received a phone call from X Group: "Huawei is a Chinese company. One day, it's going to leave, and you will never find another job. We also know where you live, we know your son's name, and where he goes to school. You be careful." G is a tough guy, and large – he is 1.95 meters tall. He joined Huawei at the end of 2007, and his professionalism and commitment have always been an inspiration to me. He didn't blink in the face of these threats. In fact, he became more determined. More than once, he told me, "No compromises."

He continued: "We are customer-centric, but that doesn't mean we always have to give in to their demands. We have to uphold the terms of our contracts and be equal partners. We have to have principles and give our customers a reason to respect us."

Dr Song told us, "You are the ones on the ground. You see what is going on, and you should trust your own judgment."

X Group was negotiating with us, but there was no good faith in their conduct. More than once, we came to an agreement, only to find the next day that they had disavowed all the commitments they had made. The team's conclusion was that we must see the case through to the end, and that there could be no further delays. We filed a new lawsuit, committed ourselves to the process, and forced it through to the bitter end. Finally, on 20 March, X Group submitted to the inevitable. We obtained a judgment from the court, demanding the central bank of country Y pay the original debt owed to us in a single payment upon receipt of the bank guarantee.

I had never felt as happy as I did the day we obtained that final judgment. Months of pressure melted away off my shoulders. The court work was not too bad – just laborious. But the negotiations had been torture. Every day my heart was hammering fit to bust, terrified that it would all be for nothing. My hair started to fall out, and my whole body seemed to twist up. G felt the same. He told me that he had been going to a temple every day, and had placed himself entirely in the hands of the gods. Looking back on it now, it does seem as though the goddess of fortune might have lent us a hand.

US$128 Million Received – Home at Last

The moment I stepped outside the court room that day, I called Dr Song and told him the good news. He reminded me that even when the court handed over the bank guarantee, our work was only 80% done. There were still risks in collection of the debt. Therefore, we should submit the payment request immediately. We could only claim success when the money was in a Huawei bank account.

Country Y has currency controls, so it's difficult to transfer large sums of money outside its borders. This meant that a cross-border payment to Huawei's bank account in Singapore required at least a two-month approval period from the central bank of Y. There was always the possibility of new variables.

The longer the process, the more the uncertainty. We were worried that something unexpected could arise.

Therefore, we found another solution. We asked the London branch of the central bank to make a payment upon receipt of the bank guarantee and transfer the money directly to Huawei's bank account in Singapore, without transferring the money first to the account of the court. This way the payment would be in real-time, efficient, and fast, without the need for approval. After a lot of lobbying from us, the London branch made a payment and transferred the money to Huawei's account in Singapore, just three days after it had received the bank guarantee.

On the morning of 9 April, R and I sat glued to the computer, constantly asking our colleagues in Malaysia whether the money had been transferred to our bank account. At 11 o'clock, the message came through that the US$128 million was now in our account. We couldn't believe it was true and asked him to check again the amount of the money and name of the payer bank. We wanted to be absolutely sure. Finally we got confirmation that it was exactly the sum named in the bank guarantee. On hearing this, the whole project team erupted in cheers and applause. We had waited so long for that moment!

Conclusion: A Miracle That Was No Miracle

It took us two years to win our lawsuit and recover more than US$100 million for the company. We, the legal affairs team, created this miracle. However, to some extent, it was not a totally unexpected one. The other two lines of Zheng Xie's poem *Bamboo and Stone* say, "Still standing strong and firm after many storms, no matter what direction the wind blows." We overcame all the difficulties and hindrances because we remained levelheaded and professional. That was how we became like tenacious bamboo ourselves, and how we won this quiet battle for the rightful assets of Huawei.

A Second Encounter

By Henry Huang Jiangning

"It is said that all encounters are a kind of reunion."

This quote, from the movie *The Grandmaster*, is a good description of my relationship with Huawei.

The first time Huawei and I encountered each other was 18 years ago. It was an interesting opportunity, but I was just preparing to head overseas and pursue my studies, so nothing came of it. I always felt a twinge of regret at what I had passed up.

Then in 2005, as I came to the end of my degree, I unexpectedly came across Huawei again, in France. This time, we seized hold of each other, and I didn't let go. I have now been with the company for the last 11 years.

Algeria: Starting with the Basics

In 2005, I graduated from HEC Paris, and joined the Huawei finance department.

Because I could speak French, the first place they sent me to was Algeria. I didn't know anything about Algeria except that it was a large country in North Africa. So I bought my plane ticket and set off, curious to see what I would find.

I was going to be in charge of collecting receivables, which sounds simple enough, but in Algeria it was actually a rather complicated business. Algerian companies were not the most efficient in the world, and our customers would take a long time processing documents. The banks were also very bureaucratic, with a lot of forms to be filled out by hand. The country also had strict currency controls. I cannot tell you how many times I was left standing at a bank counter with handfuls of forms, only to be told that I could not make any forex transactions.

When we couldn't get paid on time, our projects in Algeria would be delayed, and it was extremely frustrating. So I spent my days going between the offices of our customers and our bank manager. Before long, I'd built up strong working relationships with all of them. The pace in Algeria may not be the quickest in the world, but the people are warm and kind. Once a friendship has been established, so long as you're not asking for anything against the rules, they're always ready to help. Often, I would go and knock on a customer's door, and make my request: "Can you speed this one up for me?" And the customer would pluck the Huawei document out of the stack in their inbox, and sign it right there and then. Then I would take the completed documents over to the bank, and make the same request: "I've got all the paperwork here, could you possibly expedite the process for this one?" And once again, the bank would sort it out for me there and then.

Those first two years, I had nothing to do but devote myself to my work, and by 2006, our receivables were flowing much better than projected. That was when I won my first individual gold medal award.

Invoicing Requires Great Care

When I was in Algeria, I was in charge of another matter as well, something in theory outside of my job description: invoicing.

We didn't have a full set of finance processes working in Algeria at the time, so most of our invoices had to be issued by hand. One day, a product manager came over with a blank invoice template and asked me to fill it in for him. I was shocked: "I'm supposed to do invoices as well?"

"If you speak French, you are," he replied.

So from that day on, the job of invoicing fell to me. It didn't seem like a problem at first, but after a while, I suddenly realized how risky this process was. It made me break out in a cold sweat. All of my invoices, written by hand, were completely untraced. They weren't logged on the system. No one checked them. In fact, there was no one there who could check them, because I was the only French speaker. If one day I had a mental lapse and filled in a wrong number, then it could cause major issues.

This was a turning point! From that day on, to prevent errors, I made sure to always write out our invoices one day in advance, and left them in the drawer overnight to be checked again the next day. Even when the invoices were urgent and there wasn't time for that, I'd always put them aside for a few minutes before checking them once again. That way I was better able to spot any errors. And as it turned out, in the two years that I did our invoices in Algeria, there wasn't a single mistake.

It was a happy two years in Algeria, but there was one incident that left me feeling very hard done-by.

I had just arrived in Algeria a few months before, and I was asked to look after a group visiting from China. I had to pick them up at the airport, act as their guide, take them to meetings and dinners, and arrange their hotel... I was supposed to look after every little detail. When one of them wanted a particular type of hair dye, I scoured the city and when I finally located it, in a dusty back alley in the middle of the night, I rushed it over to the hotel. After several days running from pillar to post to serve these guys, one night I arrived back home at midnight, and I suddenly felt very sorry for myself. I'd set out to conquer the world, and here I was running around like a secretary. All of a sudden I found myself crying! Still, when I woke up the next day, I felt much better. A man adapts to his circumstances: if this was what it took to succeed here in Algeria, then this was what I would do. And I got back to my work with renewed vigour.

Henry Huang Jiangning at the Mediterranean Sea, Algeria, 2005

I did a lot of growing up in those two years in Algeria. I changed from a student into a businessman, and my responsibilities grew from receivables in Algeria to all receivables across Francophone northwest Africa.

India: Growing with the Business

One day in 2009, I was in the canteen with my manager, when he suddenly asked me a question: "The company is thinking about transferring you to India. Are you interested?" Huawei was just developing its ability to provide sales financing outside of China, and it needed people. I had returned from Algeria in 2007, and spent two years in China as a sales financing manager. I didn't hesitate: "Sure! India would be great, I've never been there. I'll go." And with that I was off on my second overseas adventure.

At that time, India was one of the fastest-growing telecom markets in the world. All of the operators were expanding, and every customer was in desperate need of financing solutions. My team would sometimes be running eight or nine separate financing projects simultaneously, and we worked with every type of customer, large and small. We were rushed off our feet.

Operator A was utterly new to project financing, and they needed us to hold their hands every step of the way, through the solution design process and the negotiations. For two years, the offices of that customer were my home from home. Operator B treated us with supreme indifference, but after tracking them for years, I spotted a rare opportunity, and developed an innovative financing exit mechanism for them. They loved it on sight: it met their strict conditions, and had Huawei's payback built in, so it was a textbook win-win solution. Yet operator C changed their mind as often as they changed their socks. They seemed to have a different idea every time I met them, and often I was left waiting in an empty meeting room for hours before someone would remember I was there and come to chat with me for a while.

There was S, rather grand and very courteous, but never giving an inch on key terms in the negotiations. And there was R, enormously wealthy but painfully stingy. They negotiated down to the last cent on every detail, and gave me headaches.

Deal by deal, we became familiar with all the pitfalls of the Indian market. Financing solutions had to be bundled with our commercial and service delivery solutions, and we needed to carefully weigh the risks and costs of Huawei, the customer, and the supporting banks. However the Indian regulatory rules were fiendishly complicated, and the market was not very well developed. Often the cost of financing was very high. On top of that, we were under a lot of pressure from competitors in India. Our customers would often push our prices down very far indeed.

What passes for public transport in rural India, 2011

We were faced with a sea of opportunities, so many that we couldn't keep up with them all. At the same time, we couldn't see clearly which would actually be profitable. The Indian market was filled with every kind of player, and some of them were past masters at fussing over details and delaying payment. But any time we failed to collect our receivables, the whole India Office was in danger of being dragged into a downward spiral.

We were exceedingly cautious about projects that needed financing among this seething mass of business opportunities. It forced us to look at all these projects from a financial perspective, to determine how we could help our sales teams design a financing solution that would take into account different types of risk. We had to learn quickly how to quantify and control risks.

I spent three years in India, and I don't regret a minute of it. My team was lucky enough to win a team gold medal during this time as well.

Growing with Our Partners

In India, we worked primarily with Chinese banks, particularly China Development Bank (CDB), in sales financing. Actually, I had started working with CDB back in Algeria. I had set up Huawei's first ever factoring deal with CDB for an order of X thousand dollars from Algeria Telecom.

I remember the first time a team from CDB came to Algeria in 2006. They didn't know anything about the country, but I had taken them to dinner, helped them find office space and hire staff.

CDB sent 80 or more teams to different countries around the world, and wherever they went, they would talk to Huawei. Our sales financing strategy was a perfect foil for CDB as it was just starting to develop an international presence. When CDB first started setting up overseas offices, it didn't have many customers at all. Huawei had a roster of large overseas customers, and we didn't stint in sharing these resources with CDB. Together we were able to build a powerful sales financing partnership.

When I came back from Algeria to Shenzhen in 2007, I worked in a financing team dedicated to CDB. During this period, the rising tide of Huawei's fast overseas expansion raised the boat of CDB as well. This allowed us to forge a powerful and positive relationship with our counterparts in the bank. For many years afterwards, even after I left Huawei's dedicated CDB team,

I would still find myself running into CDB friends working on various projects in all corners of the globe.

In the international markets, Huawei and CDB grew up together, and we felt like brothers. There was no distance between us, no "you are the company, we are the bank". There was just cooperation, snowballing under its own positive momentum.

UK: A Financial Centre Full of Undiscovered Resources

In 2012, our CEO Mr Ren Zhengfei came to speak to the sales financing team, and gave us a new direction. He said, "We need to diversify our financing resources, and work with European and Japanese banks as well... Diversity of financing resources is the key to ensuring sustainable, stable operations."

Finance Newcomer

I spent a short time working on our links with Japanese banks, then in 2013 I moved to London to help develop links with European banks. This would ensure that we could work with them to provide financing to our customers.

Huawei was a newcomer in the global financial capital of London. In 2016, we were thinking about issuing some corporate bonds, but we were undecided because we didn't have the experience or a bond credit rating. A bond specialist with 20 years of experience at a London bank told me, "In the last five years, I can only think of two or three unrated companies which have issued bonds, and they didn't get many subscribers. If you do decide to do it, you should know that it will be difficult, and you may not get the results you're hoping for."

We were extremely worried to hear this, because we really did not know exactly what we were getting into. But as we engaged more with the financial institutions of London, we began to see what was happening. The banks did not like us, not because there was a problem with the bonds we were going to offer, but simply because we were doing something new. They didn't understand this, so they didn't like it.

The company made the decision and gave the green light.

The bond issue went better than anyone had imagined. The markets lapped up our offering: there were 10 times more subscribers than predicted, and the prices were excellent. Many people at European banks said to us afterwards, "We never realized it would go this well." The banker who had warned us to be careful said that he'd never seen anything like it throughout his long career.

After this, I started to think more about myself and Huawei. Were we really still newcomers? After a while, I decided that we were not so much new as the 'new comers'. We were putting demands on the financial system that many bankers had simply never seen before.

The London finance team, 2013

Huawei's fast growth over the last few years has meant new business in every corner of the world. We have become much more widely recognized and respected, and are now a global player that the rest of the world cannot ignore. Today, it is the turn of the banks to come to seek partnerships with us.

Specialized Resources

Huawei now works in some of the most exclusive, high-end markets. But we cannot focus only on the top end. We must also remember to look after our smaller customers. As the range of our business has expanded, our customers' financing needs have become more complex. Traditional financial institutions are no longer meeting these needs.

In the London food chain, there are big fish like Citi and HSBC. But there are also plenty of nimble little minnows and shrimp. We have developed partnerships with some niche players who have rather different strategies from the big fish. Some of them seem to be a perfect match for our business strategy.

One year, when we were doing business in country B, there was some instability in the government regime. Letters of credit suddenly became impossible to be discounted. As soon as they heard the name 'B', a look of panic came over the faces of bankers. But in London we found two small banks backed by the central bank of B. We went to visit their offices, which were tiny premises in an unnoticed corner of the City of London. I wondered whether such unprepossessing institutions were really going to be able to help us. But when we sat down to talk, we found that they were extremely professional. They explained to us exactly which banks they could accept letters of credit from, and the reasons behind each one. We have now done a number of deals with these banks.

To give another example: the London insurance firm L has never defaulted in its 150-year history. It insured the Titanic. When we were helping an African customer find financing, we started by talking with L. Generally there is a lot of paperwork with government-related financing. It will often take six months or even a year to get a project going. But L was able to give us a fully-worked out answer within three days! They told us what projects they could support, and what level of support they could give. We were stunned by the speed at which they could move. With support from L, we were able to bring in another niche bank from Germany. They were willing to provide more financing, and now with this three-party team, we were able to solve the financing troubles of customers from Tanzania, Nigeria, Malaysia, and Latin America. Using the same model, we went and talked to a dozen other banks, and were ultimately able to work with three or four of them. Our financing options are growing by the day.

They say that it's horses for courses, and we have found that every kind of horse comes to race in London town. We have found all sorts of financing resources here, and put them in the service of Huawei's business. London has banks large and small; it has banks from Europe, America, and Japan.

Good Fortune and Regrets

I have often said that life is serendipity. It cannot be planned or designed.

People often ask me if I might have had a better career somewhere other than Huawei. After all, I have a degree from a top university in Paris. I know what they mean when they ask this question: If I'd gone to work in a big bank, wouldn't that have been more respectable? Wouldn't I make more money? Some of the people I studied with have gone on to become World Bank economists, IMF researchers... One guy who lived in the same hall of residence as me is now a multi-millionaire.

But I have never regretted my choice. In fact, joining Huawei was a stroke of luck for me: Huawei has given me the broadest possible stage, expanded my horizons, and made my life richer.

I never thought of working in Africa or India as a hardship. Those places made me feel alive and exhilarated. In Algeria I have seen shell fire; a bomb went off only a few dozen meters away from me. In sub-Saharan Mali I have seen big lizards in the trees in our customer's office. In neighbouring Chad, a customer took me to look at the French military base, and into the market to buy African wood carvings. I have walked through Africa's villages with my camera, and had locals crowd around me to pose in my photos. In India, I have hiked in 40 degree heat, where the soles of my shoes melted. I have flown over the endless slums of Mumbai, which were like a sea around the perimeter of the airport.

I sometimes respond to my successful university friends: I've been to places around the world that you'll never see. These are the opportunities and the experiences that Huawei gave me. How else would I ever have the chance to visit these places? I believe this from the bottom of my heart.

In London, I sit around tables with HSBC and Paribas. That's not because of my own brilliance. This is because Huawei is such a major organization, and I just happen to be Huawei's man on the ground. The platform that the company has given me has allowed me to get into the heart of the upper echelons of world finance. Gradually, step by step, I have been able to get to know this world, find its resources, and make my own contributions to the company. I believe that the work I am doing has real value. In fact, I love my job. Along the way, I've also become a minor shareholder at Huawei, and when you get to grow with a growing company, you feel more and more committed as time goes on.

Henry Huang Jiangning with Claude Trichet, former president of the European Central Bank, at Huawei ICT Finance Forum (Geneva, 2015)

Of course, you also need your employer to give you decent remuneration. But Huawei has always done that for me: my salary has enabled me to buy a flat, get married, and have a child. I may not have quite as much as some of the people I went to school with, but I have always thought that life is about more than just money. So long as you've got enough to get by, then you should think about the other aspects of a good life. Life needs breadth and depth.

However, for all these years, I have nursed one regret. In May 2005, just before I was sent to Algeria, I went to visit my parents for a few days. My father was in the late stages of prostate cancer, and he was already emaciated by the disease. I've spent a lot of time away from home, and it had never pained me to leave home before, but that time, it felt as though it was the last time I would see him. I had already walked out of the house and halfway down the road when I turned around, ran back, and embraced my father one last time. Four months later, in Algeria, I received the news that he had passed away. That was a terrible moment.

I remember in 1998, when I received a scholarship to go and study in France. I told my mother and father, who had never been outside of China in their lives, that I would use the money to take them to visit France. My father wouldn't go. He said I should save the money for a degree at a French school. I spent more than 10 years studying and working overseas, but my father never left China. Now, I will never get the chance to take him to see the places I have seen, and that is what hurts me the most. I do my best to make up for it by bringing my mother over to the UK every year to spend some time with me.

I have been with Huawei for 11 years, and all of a sudden, I'm middle-aged. Still, I plan to carry on growing with Huawei. In 2015, I was given a special award to reward my hard work all these years. The company presented me with a weighty medal, and I was honoured. For me, it did not represent an ending. Rather, it was the start of another journey, and I'm sure this one will be even more exciting.

The Swallow Flies North

By Zhong Yan

I travelled outside of China for the first time in 2012. I like to say that I was tricked into going.

I was 24, and had only been with the company for a year. I also hadn't yet found a significant other and many colleagues were saying to me, "Yan[1], you should take a chance and go on an adventure. If a young girl like you went to Africa, plenty of guys would be lined up at the airport waiting for you. You would have your pick of the lot. Why not give it a shot!"

That was how I was 'tricked' into going to North Africa.

Almost Getting Myself Lost

My first stop was Egypt. As I lugged my enormous suitcases out into the main airport hall, I didn't see a single other Chinese face. All I saw was a long line of Arab men wearing long white robes and hats standing outside the doors. At that time, Egypt had just experienced some unrest, and I was so frightened that I scurried right back into the arrivals hall. I called the regional office to arrange for a driver to pick me up.

After finally leaving the airport in a company vehicle, I looked out at the desolate scenes beyond the windows of the car as we drove. I took in each building without windows and without roofs, and my heart sunk lower and lower. Was I really going to be living and working in this sort of place? My eyes began welling up with tears. I thought of what my grandmother had said as I left: "Yan, if you don't like it abroad then come back right away. Don't worry about losing your job. If you don't have money for food, you've still got your grandmother. There isn't anything to worry about!"

Despite her kind sentiments, I couldn't bear to actually return home and live off my grandmother's kindness. I pushed back my tears, put on a brave face, and began chatting with

---

1 The name Yan in Chinese means the bird 'swallow'.

the local driver. His welcoming demeanour put me a bit more at ease. Once I arrived at my residence, I learned that it was a holiday in Egypt. With the exception of a pregnant woman, everyone in the company's Finance Management Department in North Africa had made plans, which was why only a local driver had come to pick me up from the airport.

Two days later, my vacationing colleagues finally returned, and I was invited by two colleagues to visit Egypt's largest mall, CityStar. We shopped for a while together, then got separated. The enormous mall was bustling with people, and there were countless shops and stores. I hadn't yet purchased a local SIM card, and I wasn't able to make calls using my Chinese phone.

At one point, I became separated from my new friends, and being unable to contact them by phone, I eventually started to panic. I had been on my own in the mall for over two hours. It was getting dark outside, and I was becoming more and more frightened. I walked around in circles in the mall in desperation. Just as I was about to give up hope, I saw one of my colleagues and was suddenly filled with joy. It was like I had seen a member of my own family!

Zhong Yan

My colleagues also breathed a sigh of relief, saying they had used the mall broadcasting system to call for me repeatedly. They had used English and then Chinese multiple times, but I hadn't paid attention to the broadcasts. One of them had waited at the mall entrance while the other had walked around the mall looking for me. After finally finding me, neither of them uttered a word of complaint. They worked hard to put me at ease. "Don't worry, if we hadn't found you we wouldn't have gone back. How could we leave you here on your own like that?"

In that moment, I felt bad for causing so much trouble, but also deeply moved by their kindness. It was that welcoming sentiment that gave me the determination to stay in Egypt.

Was I a Bad Deal?

After I had worked at the back office of finance in the North Africa Region for half a year, Huawei Morocco signed the largest project in North Africa – a wireless project. The former project finance manager was relocated to another position in the regional office. The local office had an urgent need for staff, and therefore my manager came to speak with me.

I had heard good things about Morocco being the "Back Garden of North Africa". My boss told me, "Morocco is a pretty nice place, but the business there is the toughest in the region. Customers there have many requirements, and the business is complex. Historically, many of the projects we signed that we thought would be profitable have turned out to be loss-makers. You've only got one week to make the job switch. The need for assistance over there is just too urgent; we need someone on that project right away..."

I don't remember what my manager said next, because I was instantly on cloud nine! I was going to Morocco! To handle project finances! As I left the meeting room my heart was soaring. I was so happy. The company was calling on finance staff to become more involved in projects. It was my view that project finance work was going to be much more interesting than the back office work I had been involved with at the regional office. I ecstatically called home right away to tell them the good news.

Who could have foreseen that a big cold bucket of water would be tossed on my enthusiasm upon meeting the General Manager of the Morocco Office.

"This is the new girl? She is going to be responsible for two major projects? We traded a highly experienced long-term employee for a young girl? Why are you always making such terrible deals?" These were the words of the general manager speaking to my boss. Even though his tone was half in jest, I could see the concern and lack of trust in his eyes.

My boss comforted me, saying that the GM had only been kidding. But I was still upset at receiving such a blow. Was I really so terrible? Was experience really all that important? I determined to make sure they knew I wasn't a bad trade!

Getting Down to Work as an Expert in 'Mine Sweeping'

In the first week in my new job, I brought everyone together for a meeting on project performance review.

In the financial system, I could see the project accounting data. I also had the estimates and budgets. I analysed the project, and listed out potential problems. I told everyone my opinion that the project was not in good shape. After I listed out the problems, I said I hoped to become fully involved in the project and figure out ways of handling the issues alongside my team members. So, I told my boss: "I want to sit with the project team." He laughed heartily. "Great," he said. "I encourage you to do that."

I had heard that contracts in Morocco had a lot of 'pitfalls'. The customer had also devised many stringent metrics that caused many contracts to become major loss-makers in execution. When I asked the project team members why the results had been so poor, they told me resignedly, "Those were the customer's requirements, so we had to sign the contract like that."

Was this true? Did the contract have to be signed like that? I was perplexed and sceptical, but didn't directly disagree with them. I knew if I questioned or blamed them without any proof, all I would do was alienate them and they would no longer be willing to talk with me. So, I decided to look at the contract myself. Whatever it is you are working on, you should always gain a full understanding before expressing an opinion.

The official language in Morocco is French, and the contract text was also entirely in French. But I only had rudimentary English under my belt, so to understand the contract I had to go online and check word-by-word, looking up everything I didn't understand. I spent more than two weeks reading through that contract line by line. I read through it until I wanted to rip it to shreds, but I eventually gained a good understanding of its contents. I also found many 'land mines' in the contract.

For example, generally a contract stipulates that customers will pay us the majority of funds after an initial acceptance inspection. Then the remaining funds will be paid several years later, after the conclusion of the warranty period. But to have such a provision for training services wasn't reasonable. Who had ever heard of a warranty period for training services? Surely it wouldn't be reasonable to provide training, then come back two years later to verify if they remembered everything? If training services also had such a warranty clause, then it would simply be impossible to receive the remaining funds.

After I read through the entire contract, I listed a series of suggestions based on the critical problems I had found. For example, I suggested that final acceptance inspection requirements not be used for training services, and that we had to avoid price transfers as much as possible.

However, reviews after-the-fact are never as effective as prevention. So, I added these key points into a 'List of Estimation Assumptions' promoted as part of the finance transformation, to be incorporated into the estimation and contract review processes for project finance. Pre-sales colleagues would look at the details of contract negotiation and reply 'Yes' or 'No' prior to my own review. If they answered 'Yes', I would look more closely at what the contract terms said. I would check what the benefits and risks were, and then quantify the data in a report to the management team for a decision.

This approach allowed us to simply and quickly identify problems, and recognize risks in advance. That List of Estimation Assumptions continued to be used even after I left my position in project finance. It basically encompassed all common 'land mines' and 'pitfalls' that could be encountered during contract signings in Morocco.

I'm Not a Leafy Green Vegetable, I'm a Hot Pepper

The success of my List of Estimation Assumptions gave me confidence, and made me feel like I was able to contribute to project finances. I was accepted and supported by the team.

Then I began to work even harder and more conscientiously in project finances. After being in Morocco for four months, I found that drive testing costs in the project were running into hundreds of thousands of US dollars. For a single site, drive testing was US$600. This was far higher than the costs of other French-speaking countries in the region such as Algeria and Tunisia. Behind the abnormal data was likely to be a problem in project management.

I looked through the drive testing framework agreement of the local office, as well as the purchase order (PO) for drive testing placed by the project team to a subcontractor. By doing so, I gradually came to understand where the issue was. During peak periods, about 250 sites would be delivered in a month. But after June, there were only about 50 site deliveries per month. The issue was that our drive testing POs were placed based on the drive testing team's costs during the peak period. After the period, we didn't release the extra POs, but continued to place POs and allow the subcontracting team to continue their work. There wasn't actually any work to be done during the off-peak periods.

On the face of things, the problem was that the project team was not monitoring PO execution, and hadn't connected resource investment with the actual workload. But after I looked into it further, the root of the problem was that the drive testing framework agreement we had signed with the subcontractor was not granular enough. There were only three ways of placing a PO: by team, by month, or by quarter. There was no way to place a PO by site, which meant it was very easy to issue too many POs.

The attention of the Deputy General Manager in charge of project delivery was piqued after I reported this issue, and the project team immediately asked the Commodity Expert Group (CEG) to discuss with the subcontractor. They eventually developed and signed a new, more reasonable, subcontracting framework agreement.

This issue made the executives of the local office aware of the importance of project finance staff. Team members also began to increasingly inquire of me about project finances. I gained more enthusiasm and momentum in my work, and soon discovered another issue: project labour costs were extremely high.

I looked through the information of the employees who had claimed work hours, and matched this up to each employee's business travel records. By doing so, I discovered that almost none of the more than 90 employees engaged during the peak delivery period was released after that time, despite the fact that delivery volume had dropped. Many people weren't engaged with the project any longer but were still on the payroll. One example of this was a former project manager who left the project over a month prior, but was still filling in work hours under the project. There were also other people who were filling in a lot of time under the project. I wrote a report to the CFO of the local office and the Deputy General Manager in charge of project delivery, informing them of the situation. I also worked with the Project Plan Control Manager to better organize information relating to delivery staff. The first thing we did was release 22 people who were no longer needed in the project. For the remaining more than 60 people, each was assigned one approver for work hours. We then reduced the number of people with approval authority from six down to two. When new people joined the project team, they had to come to my office to register before claiming work hours. After taking these measures, we got a hold of the disorderly claim for work hours.

The way I addressed these two issues caught the attention of my colleagues. Even my boss joked with me, "Nice work. I thought you were just a leafy green vegetable. Now I know you are actually a hot pepper!"

Joys of Self-growth in the Project Team

Even though my professional expertise received everyone's recognition, I was aware that to really succeed in project finances, just having a knowledge of finance was really not enough. I also had to know the specifics of business, including products and delivery.

I learned about products and various network metrics through the company's internal platform. I also consolidated what I knew from my own experience with the delivery business, and tagged along with project team members to visit sites and warehouses.

When site engineers were dismantling a site, I would use both hard and soft tactics to have them bring me along. I would stand beside them with a notebook and have them tell me about each thing that they were taking apart.

When quality management colleagues would go out to inspect a site, I would also go along with them, visiting four remote sites in a day. These colleagues were impressed that a woman was able to handle such long and tough days out on the road. When I asked them how each site was installed, I learned about how quality issues could cause adverse effects, and I would receive patient explanations to my endless questions.

Slowly but surely, I was able to more extensively participate in project management. I could provide more professional opinions, and help with project operations and risk control. Everyone's view of project finance also gradually changed, from a lack of understanding and belief that it was not useful, to recognizing the value of our work. They began to see that I could help projects make a little more money, and that everyone could receive a slightly bigger bonus.

From May 2013 when I went to Morocco, to the end of 2014 when I left my position in project finance, I was a member of the team. We saved upwards of US$10 million in project costs, effectively controlled risk, and assisted the CFO of the local office to cope with tax audits. That year and half in project finance was when I developed most rapidly within the company, and was also when I was the happiest.

As the only woman in the project team, everyone was so kind to me. At work they would answer my questions and queries, and in their off time would bring me to see beautiful scenery and eat delicious food. After they learned that I liked to hike, they would bring me to all sorts of fun mountains around the area. And I learned to make myself useful in the kitchen – something I had never deigned to do before! Very soon I became a dab hand at making dinner for everyone.

My work in project finance was great experience for me. In late 2014, I was promoted to the role of budgeting manager for the office, and I moved out of the role of focusing solely on the finances of a single project. I learned to take a wider perspective and consider the finances of the entire office.

In October 2015, I led a team in overseeing the development of the full budget for the office. With each business department, we created complete business plans and achieved a connection between business plans and strategic plans that received the recognition of the regional president. This became a template for other offices in North Africa to learn from. I have come to realize that no matter what position I hold, so long as I am proactive, conscientious, and hard-working I will be able to leverage my value, grow, and benefit. Six consecutive 'Grade A' performance ratings have given me not only more confidence, but also the courage and drive to face more challenges.

I am no longer that young girl who would cry in a difficult situation. Standing on the shores of the Atlantic Ocean and gazing out as far as the eye can see, at the horizon amidst the rolling azure waves, is the freedom only found in such wild and expansive places. As I look out at this horizon, I see my future. It's sure to be a glorious journey, one that never strays too far from North Africa.

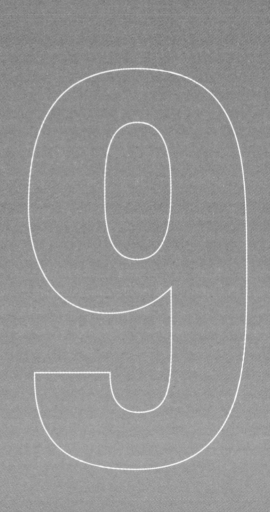

Expertise Generates Value

By Peter O'Donoghue,
Ben Binnington,
Hendrik Cornelis,
Richard Needs
and Mark Atkins

The City of London is a global financial centre. The world's most powerful and innovative financiers come here to play. Huawei's Financial Risk Control Center (FRCC) was set up in 2014, and soon after attracted many top experts in treasury, tax, accounting, and other fields of finance. They work in a high-tech office building and wield the invisible blade of finance to help Huawei in its business. Their expertise is a valuable addition to the Huawei portfolio.

My Ultimate Goal Is to Make the FRCC Redundant
By Peter O'Donoghue

During the New Employee Orientation, a video captured my attention. The video was about how Huawei installed a base station on Mount Everest. It was a very powerful video, embodying many of Huawei's core values: customer-centricity, dedication, and team work. After watching the video, as a finance professional, I thought about two questions: Where are the videos for finance in Huawei? Can we as financial professionals create value for the company like the field offices do? With these two questions in mind, I have managed to figure out two answers over the past two years: What has Huawei achieved in the past? What can I do for Huawei in the future?

Huawei has achieved some amazing things in the past. But some systematic, long-standing problems have developed, and should not be ignored. Huawei lacks end-to-end, transparent processes.

Huawei processes are very siloed and dispersed. This makes it difficult for field offices and back offices to align with each other. Lack of end-to-end synergy is not unique to Huawei. Many Western companies also face the same problem. However, Huawei's processes are more complicated than those of Western companies. Often, employees are forced to stick to the processes, and there is not the flexibility they need to align with each other.

I think Huawei can learn from some of the good practices of Western companies. If someone in a Western company feels that their corporate process is wrong, they will put the process aside and do some research. Then they will adjust the process based on what their research tells them. But Huawei employees do not have the ability to do this.

I would like to share an example from a major telecom operator I worked with before I joined Huawei. When they carried out their financial transformation project, they divided the financial staff into two groups. One group was process execution, and the other was engaged in decision support. The company wanted to strengthen the decision support side of their processes. Decision support is very important for introducing more visibility along the end-to-end process. In that company, finance staff worked alongside the business side, and were involved in every area of the business. They had both financial expertise and a deep understanding of the pain points of the business. This is why the business side valued and welcomed their advice. Huawei could draw lessons from that company.

Once the end-to-end processes are streamlined, field offices and back offices can work with each other more easily to reduce systemic risks. But there is still a long way to go. My ultimate goal may surprise you: I want to make FRCC redundant.

What does this mean? I think we can establish systems for risk prevention and provide training on methodology, so that the business side can build risk prevention and control into their work. Then the FRCC itself will no longer be important and business departments will no longer need us.

As I see it, regardless of whether we create a new product or a new system, we want it to be permanent. We cannot stay in the same position forever. We can leave only methodologies, systems, tools, and other permanent things that we have developed, to our successors. This is also true for risk control. The challenge for us is what effective methodology and tools we should develop and how we can pass them on so that they become business-as-usual at Huawei.

We are still in the early stages of this process. I have told my team that the FRCC is, in fact, creating products. Our products are not sold to our customers. They teach the business side how to analyse financial statements (balance sheet, income statement, and cash flow statement), how to look at counterparty risks using balanced scorecards, and how to analyse and mitigate tax risks.

Over the last couple of years, we have started to develop these products, but we still need to improve them, to make them replicable so that they can be used by our colleagues on the business side. Once they master these skills, the FRCC will no longer be needed.

Peter O'Donoghue joined Huawei in October 2014. He is a senior finance expert in the FRCC, Huawei's team charged with thinking outside the financial box. He is a UK chartered accountant and has a master's degree from Oxford University. He worked at Deloitte between 1990 and 2013, including 12 years as an audit partner.

Accounting Perspective: The Five Risks Facing Huawei
By Ben Binnington

I work in the Accounting Policy Center. I am responsible for reviewing financial reports to ensure that they are in compliance with accounting standards, that we are disclosing everything we have to disclose for external compliance, and that we are approving these disclosures properly.

In terms of financial information disclosure, Huawei and a Western listed company face very different requirements. Western listed companies must disclose a lot of information. It is demanded by the markets and by regulators. As a non-listed company, Huawei does not have to disclose anything.

However, Huawei has now issued bonds on the open market, though the quantities are still small. The result of such bond issuances is that we now have different disclosure obligations, and the standards that our disclosures follow are also different.

Huawei's assets are overall in a healthy state, but there are also many risks. I have studied Huawei's balance sheet, income statement, and cash flow statement, and I deal with specific transactions every day. I think Huawei faces five major risks. The first risk lies in product pricing. In the past, Huawei won market share by dint of its price advantage, but this model will not be sustainable and will create risks. The second area is market risks. Some of Huawei's products and services depend on emerging markets, but an emerging market is an inherently risky place to do business. The third risk is aggressive sales. Huawei is a customer-centric company. This is good for sales, but is risky financially because sometimes a customer's credit is not good enough. Customers might fail to pay us after we sign a contract with them, however good our internal controls might be. The fourth risk is currency risk. We don't do enough hedging. This is a fairly unique risk to Huawei. The fifth area is the effect of research and development (R&D) investment. Huawei invests heavily in R&D. But is it getting value for its money out of that expenditure? Western companies usually quantify returns from their R&D investment.

But Huawei is looking much longer term, so it often chooses to invest in technologies that will require a long gestation period.

From a financial point of view, a company needs returns on its investment. A perfect project plan should specify the budget, marketing costs, and revenue. If we cannot define all of those things, finance might block a project. My advice is, do not let finance block your way forward.

I agree that R&D investment is risky, but it is a worthwhile investment. Right now, we can afford it, and we need R&D to turn great ideas into reality. As long as there is profit, finance will not block a project just because they are concerned about the profits. Obviously, Huawei does not want to slump into a decline and shrink as an equipment maker. Instead, it wants to maintain reasonable profits and do R&D to remain as a leading company.

Ben Binnington is a UK chartered accountant and a senior accounting expert in Huawei's Accounting Policy Center. He joined Huawei in May 2014. Prior to joining Huawei, Ben worked for Barclays Bank for 10 years as the director of the accounting policy department. Prior to that, Ben worked for PwC.

Avoiding Black Swans
By Hendrik Cornelis

Huawei has many large projects. Some are worth more than US$100 million. Huawei works with many Chinese and Western financial institutions. These partners are essential to Huawei's ongoing ability to sell. If our partners cannot make money by working with Huawei, that will impact on their willingness to partner with us. If a project runs into problems (risks or less-than-expected sales numbers), Huawei will lose money. Four years ago, Huawei's non-performing assets had grown to US$3 billion, of which US$1.6 billion was Long Term Overdue (LTO) receivables. We have been resolving our non-performing assets at a rate of US$200 million each year, and the LTO total is now less than US$1 billion. But new risk exposures occur as Huawei initiates new projects. My team is responsible for collecting on our LTO receivables.

How can we effectively collect overdue receivables? The customers who fail to pay us can be divided into two categories: those who have money but are unwilling to pay, and those who do not have money. For the first category, we need to be tough. Huawei is a commercial company. We make money by selling telecom equipment and services. If Huawei cannot collect money from its customers, it cannot survive. We must make our customers understand this.

For customers who do not have enough money to pay us, our team needs to use its insight, creativity, and wisdom to work out clever solutions. Take an operator in country B as an example. When we learned that another company was going to acquire the operator, we went in to negotiate with the prospective new owner. We told them that they must first pay the operator's debts before they started the merger. Otherwise, Huawei would take further action. The company was clear that its profit from the merger would be much bigger than the US$80 million owed to Huawei. So they paid the full US$80 million in cash. In June, we received that money.

This was not our first successful collection. Three years ago, right when the FRCC was just starting up, we recovered a major debt of US$150 million. Our goal now is to recover US$200 million each year.

In addition to collecting money, our team also aims to prevent non-performing assets from emerging in the first place, by issuing early warnings and getting involved in risky projects at an early stage. When a Huawei project is at risk or may be at risk, we try to step in as early as possible. And when a project involves significant risk exposure for Huawei and our financial partners, we monitor payments and the financial health of our customers from end to end.

We never make snap decisions. All risk warnings are driven by data and analysis, not by subjective judgments. Every time we make a decision, we conduct a full investigation, visit the customer, and finally output a risk report. We also have good relationships with bankers, lawyers, and consultants, so we can work with them to analyse current and expected revenues, cash flow, markets, and liabilities. If a customer makes its revenue in soft currencies, but its liabilities are in hard currencies, we need to pay special attention to that customer. Because in our experience, this is a significant risk factor.

But it is frustrating when our risk warnings are ignored by field offices. Take country A as an example. In 2015, we learned that one of the country's operators was struggling because of a mismatch between its soft-currency revenue and its liabilities, which were in hard currencies. We sent a warning to the Huawei office in country A: "This operator is in trouble, and it is likely to go bankrupt."

At that time, the local office was very angry about our warning. They thought that this operator was the largest in the market, and there was no way it could go bankrupt. We sent the office a detailed report, showing what was going on with the operator, but they still would not accept it. As it turned out, the operator filed for bankruptcy not long later.

My biggest concern is actually 'black swans'. We have to ask "What if…" all the time.

What kind of event would really destroy Huawei? If we have payment problems in a small country, we will lose hundreds of millions of dollars. That's a blow, no doubt, but Huawei can survive such an event. But if an accident happens to a major operator, or to a major country or region, it could pose an existential risk to Huawei. That could be a real Waterloo for us. Regardless of the probability of this risk (even if it is a very low probability), we have to think about it, because of the seriousness of the impact if it should happen. We have to know in advance what the situation will be for Huawei if a particular project starts losing money. As financial experts, we can provide support and advice for our local offices, and offer solutions to help them solve issues and control risks.

Hendrik Cornelis joined Huawei in February 2013 as the director of the Non-performing Asset Management Department. He graduated from Harvard Law School, and is a licensed lawyer. Prior to joining Huawei, he served as the head of technology, media, and telecoms at ING's investment banking division.

Minimizing Exposure to Tax Risks
By Richard Needs

Compliance Does Not Mean No Risk

In the early years, Huawei's tax department only worked on compliance: Are we paying the right taxes? Are we filing the right tax returns? This was all Huawei needed at the time. But as Huawei has grown from an unknown outsider to an industry giant, the tax risks facing the company have increased. There has also been a global shift in how international tax is managed. Huawei has to change its philosophy on tax and introduce the concept of financial risk controls.

In 2014, Huawei set up the FRCC in London. I have worked in the FRCC's Tax Risk Control Department since then, and have served as the director of the department since March of this year. We focus on how to help Huawei identify and quantify tax risks.

What are the tax risks facing Huawei? After getting familiar with Huawei's business and processes, I found that our core value of customer-centricity has helped Huawei grow by leaps and bounds, but it has also created some tax risks. Huawei puts the customer first. As a result, we may make non-standard changes to contracts, products, or services to cater to customers. But from the perspective of tax, different entities are subject to different tax policies and regulations. If we blindly put the customer first, we may damage our own interests.

But this is not to say that our business side always has to put tax risk ahead of sales. The key is to understand how much tax risk we are prepared to bear, and for the tax team to develop policies and business models to deal with that risk.

Therefore, the challenge for our team is to work with the HQ management team and the tax team to identify, analyse, and quantify tax risks; to find effective solutions; and to provide advice for field employees so that they can strike a balance between business development and tax risk mitigation.

Sometimes the business side is not very open to these suggestions. They say, "We are very experienced. We have been doing things this way, and never had a problem. Why should we change it now?" But the truth is that Huawei's business has grown and tax systems are much more complicated than before. So our past experience is not very applicable to our present situation.

Take another leading tech company as an example, which I will call company X. It was ordered to pay a EUR13 billion tax bill by the EU, and it was not even aware that its business model put it at risk. In the past decade, they have complied with the law and there have been no problems. So they assumed that there was no problem with their business model. But the EU still ordered company X to pay EUR13 billion in back taxes.

Tax risks do not appear overnight. They build up over time. Huawei should learn the lessons of companies like company X. We have always complied with the law, but that does not mean that no risks exist.

Creating a Risk Map

How should we identify, analyse, and quantify risks, to avoid repeating past mistakes?

At present, we do not have a unified set of standards for identifying tax risks. But we have established a model to identify high-risk countries. The model looks at multiple factors, including the number of employees, sales revenue, profit, and the complexity of our business model in the country. For example, if Huawei is doing a wide range of business in a country, including R&D, management, and services, then the risks that Huawei faces in that country are higher than in countries where we have only a single type of business (such as sales via a distributor).

This model can help us work out which countries to start on with our analysis. On the basis of the model, we can develop a risk map to identify the risks which occur in multiple countries. We call these common risks.

Common risks are of particular interest to us. The Huawei leadership and HQ tax team should work together to identify the severity of these risks, decide whether they are acceptable, and work out solutions. Other risks can be addressed on a case by case basis.

We are developing a tax risk control process. We plan to have the framework in place within three years, and then spend another year or two refining it. The framework is a little bit like this room I am in. We can start to hang one picture on a wall and hang the second picture on another wall. We can then position the tables. We can bring each element together one after another. We should start with the important elements. Everyone has to contribute their ideas about which are the most important issues, in alignment with Huawei's long-term goals and vision. Otherwise, the risk framework ends up just like an empty shell, without the content required for effective risk control. This risk framework needs to be applicable in day-to-day business decisions and tax compliance activities before it can effectively control risk. This sets a high bar on the design of the framework. If the framework is unworkable or does not fit with the way we do business, then it is just a castle in the air.

Richard Needs joined the FRCC's Tax Risk Control Department in September 2014 as a direct tax expert. He worked at PwC and Vodafone for 17 years, in the areas of corporate tax, tax risk management, tax compliance, and tax audit. He has extensive experience in corporate tax management in multinational companies.

Understanding Culture and Retaining Talent
By Mark Atkins

I worked in the investment banking industry for 20 years before moving into the telecom industry. Before joining Huawei, I worked in finance management at Motorola for 10 years. When I joined Huawei as a sales financing expert, I helped the company grow the sales financing business from scratch. At that time, there were no overseas experts in my position, so I felt like a bit of a lab rat. No one knew how we should develop the business or whether we could succeed.

After two years in sales financing, HQ asked me to lead a pilot team to develop the global credit risk business. I helped Huawei establish the London Center of Expertise for Credit, which later evolved into the FRCC. I have worked at Huawei for more than nine years. People ask me why I have chosen to stay at Huawei for such a long time. I think it all comes down to my months of experience in China.

During that time, I was able to learn a lot about Chinese culture, by attending social events and sightseeing around the country. I integrated myself into the local culture and society, and looked at the Chinese people and Huawei's corporate culture from a new perspective. Now, I can see the gaps between Chinese and Western culture, and I can appreciate the differences.

I would like to share an example of business culture. In 2010, Huawei had a record year in terms of profits. Everybody was very excited because they got big bonuses. However, Huawei's CEO Mr Ren Zhengfei said that he was very upset. Why was he upset when Huawei was making large profits? He explained that fantastic profits meant that Huawei had charged its customers too much. In other words, Huawei had taken money from our customers that they could have used to grow their business. Mr Ren Zhengfei looked at Huawei's success from the perspective of the entire ecosystem. He was concerned about the business success of Huawei and our customers, whereas Western companies only care about their own success (and that success is often achieved at the expense of others). I was inspired by Mr Ren Zhengfei's philosophy and shared it with my non-Chinese peers. They gradually came to understand the differences between Chinese and Western business culture.

I would like to say something about HR management at Huawei. This is not about non-Chinese professionals, but the Chinese talent which Huawei spends a lot of time and money cultivating.

I've seen some Chinese colleagues leaving Huawei in their 30s, just as their careers should be taking off.

I think sometimes that people do not feel cared for, and that is why they leave Huawei. They feel that the company does not care about their future career development, or that the company is not giving them opportunities to fully unlock their potential. If we compare the company to a family, conflicts, arguments, and setbacks are inevitable. But family members do not feel hurt just because of the occasional dispute. We have to show our colleagues that we care about them, even if we sometimes do not like them. Over the past two years, Huawei has made great progress in employee care. The voice of staff is heard and understood much better, and a better organizational climate has been built for talent cultivation and retention, so that all staff, especially middle managers, can feel cared for. To make employees feel cared for, we should provide both monetary and non-monetary incentives. It is not just financial rewards. We show love to our children by making them feel like they are part of the family, instead of giving them sweets. The company should give employees support and encouragement and help them unlock their potential. Money is very important, but it is not everything. There is always somebody somewhere who will offer you more money to leave. What keeps people at Huawei when other companies offer them more money? It is a sense of belonging. People who choose to stay, if other companies offer more money, are those who really love Huawei. But Huawei first has to make them feel cared for, so that they are willing to stay here.

A high salary is not the only reason that employees want to stay at Huawei. A sense of accomplishment matters more than pay.

Huawei is a winning team. Everyone wants to share the glory of its success and be a member of that team. I would like to share a story from when I worked at Motorola, about a competition between Motorola and Huawei. Although we had smart people, good systems, and efficient operations, we still lost a project to Huawei. There was a lot of frustration about that! This story tells us that success is the mother of success. Huawei has become a successful company. If Huawei can let its employees grow with it, and provide them with a clear, satisfactory career development path, then our staff will be more willing to stay.

If Huawei wants to maintain success in the long run, it must pay attention to talent cultivation and retention. Today's young people are the leaders of tomorrow. If Huawei is willing to support, nurture, and retain its most outstanding employees, and help them realize their ambitions, it will have stronger leaders in the future. These leaders will make greater contributions and leverage their experience, knowledge, and skills to take Huawei to the next level.

Mark Atkins worked at Motorola for more than 10 years. Prior to that, he worked at Canadian Imperial Bank of Commerce (CIBC), CIBC Wood Gundy, Deutsche Bank, Morgan Grenfell, and Citibank.

Young Girl with Big Ideas

By Ariella Ji

A Unique Work Report

One day in 2009, the outgoing CFO of Huawei Vietnam took me to meet the general manager. On the GM's face, I read distrust. "She might be the CFO now, but if the Vietnam Office runs into any problems, I still want you to come and sort it out!" he instructed my predecessor. I could read between the lines: Why have they sent a 29-year-old girl to be my CFO?

I could understand why he didn't trust me. His new CFO had a degree from a good university, three years as a KPMG auditor, and four years in the back office of Huawei finance, and that was it. I had never worked in a field office, and suddenly I had been parachuted into Vietnam, which was one of Huawei's top 10 offices by revenue. They called it 'Little India', because it was nearly doing as well as the very successful India Office.

I bit my tongue. I thought: I will prove myself in the end!

A few months later, the Vietnam Office organized a work report. When I was preparing my presentation, I read finance reports from other offices and found that they all focused on finance: various financial metrics and whether they were on target; how finance handled budgeting and forecasting; how finance dealt with expense claims... None of these reports looked at finance from a business perspective.

After some thought, I decided to include something different in my report. First of all, I tried to use the language of the business side, not just financial figures. Secondly, I tried to look at business operations, to see where our problems were and where our opportunities lay. I was looking to create greater value for the business.

On the day of the meeting, the finance report was, as usual, placed last on the agenda. The earlier speakers overran their time slots, so by the time it came to my turn, it was already 5:30pm Everyone's mind was on dinner, rather than my presentation. And of course, the sales managers weren't interested in finance anyway. They believed that finance was just about keeping the books, dealing with payments, and handling expense claims. Our work didn't have anything to do with them.

I didn't take their indifference to heart. I presented my report as planned. I started by telling everyone that the finance report should really be second on the agenda, right after the general manager, not last thing in the day. I didn't talk about payments and expense claims at all. I talked about how the Vietnam Office was going to hit its targets next year. We had three really large customers who made up the bulk of our orders in Vietnam, and I laid out targets and plans for each of them. I talked about how we should finish the projects already underway, when we should be signing the customers up for new projects, and what sort of margins we needed on new projects. For each of the three key account departments, I explained the core tasks and timetables. And I made full use of my time slot. I didn't skimp on the detail just because everyone else was keen to get out of the office.

The president of Huawei Southeast Asia, who was at the meeting, seemed very excited. He praised my presentation and said this was how finance reports should be done. He liked my operational ideas as well. There and then he changed the agenda for these meetings: The general manager would talk about our recent performance and the local market, then the CFO would speak on internal, operational matters and lay out new rules.

At the company dinner after that meeting, I was moved from the second table to the top table. That evening, everyone came up to toast me. I had finally got my feet under the table – both in the company, and at the restaurant!

Brazening My Way into the ST² Meeting

Actions speak louder than words. I knew that I had to do something to show that our finance team could create value for business.

At that time, the Vietnam Office was doing a turnkey project in which we were building an entire new network for customer H.

---

2 The Staff Team manages day-to-day operations in a Huawei local office.

We also had several other smaller turnkey projects running at the same time. I noticed that between April and October every year, our projects seemed to progress very slowly, and it seemed to be slowing our revenue. Every time we talked about this slow revenue growth at meetings, I used to get a stack of excuses about why the revenue wasn't coming in. Something felt strange, so I went and talked to a Vietnamese colleague. He immediately solved the mystery for me: "That's the rainy season in central and southern Vietnam."

I asked him, "Can't we build during the rainy season?"

"You grew up in a city, didn't you?" he answered in astonishment.

The central and southern regions of Vietnam have a tropical climate and are largely rural. Days of heavy rain will make the soil very unstable, which makes it impossible to do any construction work. The rainy season there is totally different from what I had experienced in my hometown in eastern China.

During the rainy season, all building work had to be shelved. And when the rain was heavy, all outdoor activity had to stop. As a result, our projects were getting bogged down.

With this knowledge, I talked to our delivery managers about the possibility of varying the pace of our projects. During the dry season, we had to do as much work as possible, and we would hire as many contractors as we needed. Then during the rainy season, our key account teams would talk to the customers about spending the time getting in stock and making preparations. In the meantime, we could pause the construction work, and put our contractors on furlough. This would help speed up project progress and improve our financial performance.

This experience has taught me that finance absolutely needs to understand the business side, including what's happening on the ground. It's no good just assigning tasks and giving commands without a full grasp of what you're doing.

The best way to understand the business of the office in the shortest time possible is through attending the staff

We need to learn more about the business side if we want the company to see the value we provide. If the finance department doesn't understand the business the company is doing, then of course no one will think that the work we do is important.

team meetings. At that time, CFOs were not required to go to ST meetings. But I saw them as an excellent opportunity, so I decided to go to the meeting even if no one asked me. I found out the time and location of the meeting, and went in 15 minutes ahead of time.

As everyone came into the meeting room and saw me, their surprise was obvious. They seemed to be wondering why on earth I was there. I explained that I wanted to learn about the business side, as it would be helpful for my own work. I could see everyone was still a bit worried, so I added, "I'm the CFO. I have to see all confidential documents anyway. And I'm only here to listen, not to talk." Only then did everyone relax and laugh, which meant I could stay. Since then, I have become a fixture at ST meetings.

I often tell my colleagues that we need to learn more about the business side if we want the company to see the value we provide. If the finance department doesn't understand the business the company is doing, then of course no one will think that the work we do is important.

An End to Low Prices

In 2012, I became the CFO of Huawei Southeast Asia. One day, the general manager of Huawei Thailand approached me with a question: "What's your reason for proposing such a high quote?"

He was referring to the price for site maintenance in the quote we were putting together for a major project. He thought that my suggested price was too high. For several years now, the Thailand Office had provided these maintenance services at cost price to make sure we could always win the contract. In 2012, I suggested that we raise the price and no longer aim to pick up market share with low prices.

I replied to him, "This is just my suggestion. We will all discuss it together before we decide on the quote." Right there and then I called the regional vice presidents in charge of solutions and project delivery to come and discuss it with us.

"Let me explain my reasoning, then we can make a decision." After all, I wasn't just plucking this price out of the air. I had good reasons.

My judgment was that our customers expected us to complete large projects fast, and to a high level of quality. In Thailand, Huawei had relationships with the best contractors, so we could build base stations twice as fast as any of our competitors. Of course, high quality inevitably means higher costs. I had based all of these ideas on the annual reports delivered by the Thailand Office.

If we were to offer the same price as our competitors, and our service were better, then our costs would also be higher. So how were we going to make money on it? And if we didn't make money, then how would the Thailand Office and the key account departments survive? How could we keep hold of our partnerships with contractors?

Of course, we could continue to quote low prices. That seemed to make the customer happy, of course. But if our low prices meant that we couldn't deliver the high quality, then in reality, we were getting things backwards. That was not really what the customer wanted. And our relationship with our customers shouldn't be about low prices and quick sales. If we wanted sustainable partnerships with our customers, we should be setting reasonable prices and delivering high-quality services.

When I'd said my piece, everyone said that they'd go and think it over, and in fact they very quickly accepted my suggestion and bumped up our service prices considerably. After we submitted our bid, everything went surprisingly smoothly: the customer agreed to our new price without hesitation. This was in line with my reasoning that our customers care most about quality, and that they know that high quality means higher cost. Our customers were willing to pay more for better services.

The profits from this project came like sunshine on a rainy day for Huawei Thailand – in fact for the whole of Huawei Southeast Asia. Between 2010 and 2011, we had won a lot of projects with very low quotes in order to gain market share. Now, in 2012, as those projects wrapped up, we were losing money and had declining revenues. Our local offices were also being asked to set aside some budget to support Huawei's two new business lines: enterprise and consumer. They were having a difficult time.

How can we strike a balance between profits, strategic market share, and new business development? This was a question that needed the special attention of a CFO. I offered several suggestions which were accepted by the regional management. We looked at the projects we had taken on for the sake of market share, and which weren't making any money, then we directed more resources towards the best of them and imposed strict budget controls on the others. We also sent more resources towards some of our less strategic, more profitable projects. We changed the way we used Huawei HQ expert resources, which the region had to pay for. Previously, we had brought in a lot of HQ experts, and kept them in the region despite the extra cost, because we didn't want to lose them. Now we required all project teams to define exactly which experts they needed, and we sent the rest home. Project teams were made responsible for their own budgets and how they are executed. Their bonuses depended on the financial performance of the projects. This comprehensive package of criteria helped us to run a tighter ship and improve performance.

There is an old saying: adversity reveals genius. If a company is able to maintain big margins without any difficulty, I think it probably doesn't need a CFO. Looking back now, my years in Thailand and Southeast Asia were the years I learned more than at any other time, because I was forced to dig deep into the details of our operations.

Putting My Head on the Chopping Block

In the first half of 2013, a telecom operator was planning to build a new network in a new country, 'M'. The contract was worth more than US$1 billion, and involved a five-year turnkey contract to build the network, and an eight-year managed services contract to maintain it afterwards. Both Huawei and a Western competitor were desperate to win the contract. At Huawei, our project sponsor was Ryan Ding, a board member.

This was a huge contract. If we could win this contract, it would mean a massive gain in our market share. We wanted that contract badly, but the team was divided over the price. Some said we should quote a price lower than that of the competitor. I was arguing that we should bid higher. I understood that a higher price could lead to failure: the customer would rank bidders by order of price – from low to high – and negotiate with them one by one. If they reached an agreement with a bidder with a lower price, they would not even talk to other bidders.

A high price could end up with us being knocked straight out of the tender, but I had good arguments on my side. First, Huawei was more capable and experienced than our competitor in terms of building networks in that country, especially in remote areas. Our strength should be reflected in our price. I also identified a strength that no one else had spotted: country M had strict foreign exchange controls. Our competitor did not have a subsidiary or any legal entity in-country, which meant that it was not able to transfer local-currency payments back to HQ, or to transfer significant sums of money into the country in US dollars. They simply didn't have any way to accept or make the large payments that this project would require. Unlike them, Huawei had a subsidiary there and had means to transfer our money. This was a selling point for us.

We could offer high-quality delivery and financial convenience. Naturally, that meant higher costs for us. If we chose to position ourselves as a pure price competitor with a low quote, then even if we won the contract, where would we be making our profits over the next few years? If we couldn't build reasonable profits into this contract, then how could we continue to provide the customer with high-quality services?

Based on this analysis, I insisted that we quote a higher price than our competitor. I told my colleagues that if they rejected my advice, I would veto the bid, and the issue would be escalated to the Huawei Group CFO.

My intransigence caused quite a stir. There were even ugly rumours behind my back: "Ariella is about to transfer back to HQ", they said. "She doesn't care if we get this contract or not." Half of that rumour was true. I was about to transfer out of Southeast Asia. But in fact, that was all the more reason for me to just say yes to the lower price. If the region was unable to make any profits, it would have no impact on me. My salary and bonus wouldn't be coming from the Southeast Asia region any more. I could have been remembered as a jolly good fellow, and avoided all of this backbiting. But I was the regional CFO. I knew that it was my job to put my foot down on this issue. I had to tell honestly what my judgment of the situation was, rather than worry about whose toes I might be stepping on. Sometimes, if you know something is right, stepping on a few toes is just something you have to live with.

Fortunately, Ryan Ding supported my suggestion. He made his decision: "We are stronger than our competitor in many respects, and that should be reflected in our price. This is the price we should ask. Why would we accept anything less?"

The bids were opened. Our price was higher than that of our competitor, so they got first bite. However, they were unable to meet the financial conditions that the customer was demanding, so the customer ended the negotiation and turned to us.

Our talks ran on for several days. At around 4am on the very last day of the negotiations, the customer demanded that we denominate the contract and accept payment in the local currency. If Huawei accepted this condition, they said, they would award us the contract there and then.

At that time, the local currency in M was depreciating rapidly. The project would last for years, and M was a newly opened market. There were a lot of unknowns ahead, and this new condition would mean that a huge chunk of our project profits would be eaten up by exchange rate fluctuations. But the customer wouldn't budge. As CFO, it was down to me to come up with a financial solution. To solve a problem, you have to put yourself in the customer's shoes. We talked with them again and again, and finally we learned the real driver behind this demand: the customer's subsidiary in country M was making profits in the local currency that the customer couldn't find any way to spend.

Now that we understood their real problem, everything else was easy. I made two suggestions. First, we could denominate the equipment contract in US dollars, and the services contract could be in the local currency. After all, Huawei needed local currency revenue as well, to pay our local contractors. Second, we built exchange rate protections into the agreement. The contract needed to state that the exchange rate between the local currency and the US dollar must be updated on a quarterly basis. The customer said they had to talk to their management at HQ. One hour later, they agreed to our proposals, and the huge contract was finally ours!

No Boxes or Boundaries

It has been more than three years since I left Huawei Southeast Asia and joined the Subsidiary Finance Management Department, part of the Huawei Group Finance Management Department. So far, I've been with Huawei for 12 years. I never imagined that I would stay at Huawei for this long.

Before I joined this company, I thought it was provincial and backward. In Shanghai, the KMPG office was in the same building as Huawei Shanghai, so I ran into Huawei staff sometimes. They didn't look like the rest of us. We were prim office belles, mostly employed by non-Chinese companies. The Huawei guys didn't seem to care about their appearance. They didn't even wear suits when they were interviewing new candidates. Our office building only had a sandwich shop downstairs, which the rest of us made do with. The Huawei team would order in stacks of steaming Chinese food. In the local restaurants, if one company had negotiated a staff discount, some Huawei staff would beg use of someone else's company card to get 10% off.

But this backward, provincial company was able to give me a very tempting job offer, and so I boarded a plane from Shanghai to Huawei HQ in Shenzhen. I had only just finished the boarding process when I was told that my job had been filled by someone else! Instead, they were placing me in the operations support team (now the quality and operations team), part of the finance department. They told me that this was not uncommon at Huawei, and that my salary wasn't being cut, so it was really all the same. I was not happy. "All the same! Every person's career is different."

But I didn't leave, because I had two goals. The first was to learn about business operations and finance management in practice. The second was my next career goal: to become a finance manager. I hadn't achieved these goals; it was still the same company that I had chosen to work for, so I might as well stick it out a little longer, right?

If the company was going to place me in the operations support team, then that's what I would do, and I would do it well. If I could excel in a job that I had no interest in, wouldn't that prove that I was an impressive team player? Back then, operations support was a tough job. The processes had not yet been set up, and many departments weren't interested in working with us. Often, I had to rack my brain for new ways to nudge my managers and colleagues around to my way of thinking.

I have always had a can-do spirit, and the way I ensnare people can be a bit unusual. I was often seen standing outside the men's room, waiting for the vice president of the Finance Management Department. I was a familiar face – and the only woman – in the smoking room, where male managers in the finance team often gathered to discuss work. By working that way, I could kill many birds with one stone.

Before I joined the company, I was told that its corporate culture was very unusual and regimented. After working here for some time, I have found Huawei to be very open and inclusive. For example, I have never had a negative reaction to my can-do style. Everyone accepts and even supports me. The company doesn't expect you to be perfect, nor does it demand a fixed approach to work. You can be as different as you like. So long as you do good work, it will be recognized.

Later, during my four years overseas, I increasingly came to believe that my untrammeled style was mirrored by the company's ethos. If I had not pushed my way into those ST meetings in Vietnam, then I would never have learned so much about the business and been able to suggest relevant new ideas. If I had accepted a low-price strategy for key projects in Thailand, then my vision of "finance steering the business" would have been meaningless. During the bid in country M, if Ryan Ding had waved me off to the sidelines, where the finance team has traditionally languished in Huawei, then I would have handed in my letter of resignation.

Huawei is totally different from my previous employer, a Western company. In that company, everyone had their own patch of ground to take care of. They just had to do their own work. There was no 'upside' to breaking down barriers. At Huawei, there are no individual patches of ground, and there are no ceilings. It's like being a seed in the earth: no one tells you how to grow, and the company doesn't lay stones so that you can only grow in certain ways. There is plenty of open space, no boundaries or limits, so if a seed is willing to push through, it can have as much earth as it wants. It can grow as high as its own limitations will allow. It's entirely up to you, and how hard you are willing to push.

If you are ready to push the envelope, stake your claim on the world, and take on responsibility, then you will receive support and appreciation. When we push the limits, our colleagues and managers do not shut us down for getting too big for our boots. They invite us to sit at the table with them.

Maybe this culture is what makes Huawei so attractive. Generations of Huawei pioneers have thought and invented outside the box, and inspired the next generation by creating opportunities for them, embracing and encouraging them, and leading by example. This is what has created today's Huawei in all its vibrancy, and I am proud to be a part of it.

Embracing Cooperation Along the Shores of the Vistula River

By Hongbin

The Poland financing team fell into silence when they received the task. The words "Poland S Corporation" flickered as they were projected onto the screen, as did the mood of the team, between excitement and doubt. The team was elated to have the incredible opportunity provided by the project, but also concerned about potential risks...

A Project Developed from Scratch

The mobile network operator 'S' was first established in Poland in 2006. In its early days, S was the fourth largest mobile operator in Poland, and most other players in the market didn't pay much attention to the company. However, the 'new kid on the block' was ambitious and had ideas about catching up to the pack. S wanted to build a 3G network of its own as the local 2G networks were in the process of evolving into 3G. This was not only creating space for S to survive, but giving the company the opportunity to overtake the competition on the inside track.

During this time, the European 2G market was dominated by US and European companies, whereas 3G was only just emerging as a field of business. Huawei was seeking an opportunity to expand, and noted that the strategy of S was consistent with our own plan to establish a showcase project and make a breakthrough into the 3G market. The aims of both companies to break into the market coincided nicely.

This was why Huawei was able to build a relationship with S before any US or European companies had noticed this newcomer. Nevertheless, as a newly established company, S needed both technical and financing solutions from its partners, and the latter was often more critical.

Usually, commercial banks are not willing to invest in a newcomer that has no major holdings. It might have been fate that brought S, Huawei, and China Development Bank (CDB) together, as the business needs of the three parties perfectly matched up. This was the chance that S had been waiting for to obtain financing.

However, the shareholders of S were two private equity firms that couldn't provide strong parent company guarantees for their financing, which would amount to hundreds of millions of euros. There were also numerous uncertainties relating to the fact that the project was starting from scratch. This meant that there was a lot of work to do to get things off the ground, including building networks, acquiring users, and developing the business.

Would it be possible to provide financing to S? The reality was that because of the high risks attached to the project, it was hard to gain direct financing from an overseas financial institution. Even CDB, which had extensive experience dealing with foreign financing projects, had concerns regarding this project. These complications were increasing the pressure felt by Huawei.

Clarifying Things from Every Possible Angle

Li Jia'nan was the financing manager at the time, who had professional knowledge of finance but had little practical experience. He was worried about such a challenging project.

Some proven practices could be learned from the perspective of sales financing. The first important task was to look into various aspects such as the macro economy, market size, and policy environment in Poland. We also had to examine the company's development strategies, shareholder investments, and the experience of executives. Moreover, we had to be willing to take risks and make tough decisions.

Together with the account manager, Li evaluated the project before he made a final decision. Li and the account manager travelled extensively to gain more information, including a trip to the Office of Electronic Communications (UKE). They carried out countless interviews with staff from major operators and citizens as potential network users. They also learned more about the company through frequent phone calls and on-site visits. Huawei's investigation was so detailed that employees from S began to sigh, "Seriously, we've already told you everything we know!"

After gaining greater insight through investigation and analysis and with the guidance of HQ colleagues, we came to the conclusion that the project was of strategic significance to our business, and also had good prospects in regards to financing.

Poland's economy was doing very well. The telecommunications policies of Poland were stable and standardized under the EU framework, and the three major operators maintained a balance in the market and were making enormous profits. Most importantly, we learned that the UKE intended to introduce a new competitor and was offering favourable policies aimed at invigorating the market.

We saw that S could be that competitor. Although the shareholders of S were private equity firms, their investment management teams had some experience in telecom investment and their business plans were highly practicable. More importantly, a considerable amount of equity capital was expected to be added to the investment after our negotiations. All of these factors suggested that financing for S was feasible.

Based on our judgments, the financing team and the local sales team made several reports to Huawei headquarters. Finally the executives agreed that the project was feasible and that potential risks could be taken to support the development of S. The time to play our hand had come.

In October 2006, mid-Autumn in Poland, Huawei, CDB, and S fully embraced the idea of cooperation. The first round of contracts and financing agreements were signed and the network was rapidly deployed. The injection of financing invigorated the process like a stone thrown into a tranquil lake.

In March 2007, S's network was launched for commercial use and had acquired over 3% of the market share within a year. This achievement immediately pointed to the fact that the financing decision was a wise one. The decision had enabled Huawei to achieve a breakthrough in the European 3G market.

We did what
we did in order to
make the financing
more professional
and reasonable.

'Bundling' Us Together

The initial successes strengthened our confidence, and in June 2008, we signed a second round of contracts and financing agreements. S saw its customer base grow dramatically, and the successful financing was one of the most important contributing factors. Mr Jorgen, the CEO of S, stated in a meeting at the time: "As Liza May Minnelli's song goes, 'money makes the world go around', and that's also the case between us three partners."

However, concerns remained about whether the loan of hundreds of millions of euros could be totally recovered in the future.

More had to be done to mitigate the potential risks. We couldn't just give money to customers and leave it at that. Therefore, although evaluation and analysis had been conducted to make the financing decision, additional conditions also had to be made with the customer.

In the second round of financing, we decided to separate the funds into two parts. A relatively large amount of money was separated as standby credit, which could only be used when the assumptions of business plans panned out. The customer initially disagreed with this decision and tempers even flared at some points. The customer complained, "Why shouldn't we be able to decide how and when to use the money that has been financed to us?"

We did what we did in order to make the financing more professional and reasonable. We explained, "We are doing this to protect the interests of everyone involved. We want to make sure S is able to develop in a robust and stable manner. We hope that S will consider the risks that exist in development and ensure that operations gradually unfold. The better that S develops, the more valuable the financing will be."

We also asked S's shareholders to fulfill their commitment to add equity capital prior to the financing agreement taking effect, and to provide a certain amount as a standby investment fund in the event that funds were needed. This ensured that there was a level of risk for S, encouraging them to use the funds more prudently.

These measures enabled us to ensure there was collateral on hand as well as financial discipline. It also made customer shareholders more involved in the project. S's shareholders, who had extensive experience in investment, couldn't help but praise the approach, saying, "Yes, that's the professional way to do it."

In fact, all of these measures acted as a safety rope. It seemed that S was limited by certain restrictions, but the safety rope provided by these measures reduced the risk of 'falling from the cliff'. In this way, the risks faced by Huawei and CDB could be controlled and S could develop in a more stable manner.

"We're Going to Be Number One!"

The market share of S reached 12% in early 2011, and its cash flow was going to be tight if S was to develop further.

However, S's loan balance with CDB had reached an all-time high. It was hard to decide whether to provide additional financing to further support S's development or to tighten the financing to mitigate the risk exposure.

We further analysed S's business plan. We also asked a financing expert and a credit expert, who were both supporting financing projects in Eastern and Northern Europe, to help us conduct a stress test based on S's business plan and relevant data. We made some conservative assumptions of the company's operating data and results, and used the assumptions to infer possible scenarios. The stress test showed that the development space for S was still large and the principal and interest could be paid off even if unfavourable situations arose within an assumed reasonable range.

Would CDB be willing to provide further financing? It was decided that direct communication between the three parties would probably be the most effective way to solve the problem. With this in mind, in the spring of 2011, we planned for S's executives to discuss the issue with CDB executives in Beijing.

"We have cooperated successfully. Now 4G is about to hit the market and represents a remarkable opportunity for us," stated one of S's executives in the meeting with CDB. "S is developing with stability and it won't have a problem paying off the principal and interest in the future," added a representative from Huawei.

The room became quiet as everyone waited for the CDB executive to make a decision. Finally, the executive said, "We hope to continue this beneficial cooperation." As the meeting was wrapping up, one CDB executive joked, "We hope S won't be content with its current status. Maybe you can move ahead to the calibre of top operators." This brought peals of laughter and applause.

"Moving ahead to the calibre of top operators" was just wishful thinking for S at the time. However, S didn't take this as a joke, and seriously considered how they could make it a reality. Several days later, a 'Top Operator Business Plan' was presented to Huawei and CDB. S was setting the ambitious goal of becoming the top industry player in Poland!

As a new operator, it had already been difficult for S to gain a foothold in the market and to develop as well as it had. Was becoming the top player in the industry just wishful thinking? At least we thought so.

Pulling It All Together for the Customer

S set a more ambitious plan and raised its financing requirements by hundreds of millions of euros.

"It's a little crazy, isn't it?" asked the then financing manager Zhang Hongbin and the team in Poland. We could see that additional financing was necessary, since there was still significant space for S to develop. Nonetheless, we were aware that the excess investment might end up causing more harm than good. We decided that the financing requirements needed to be reduced.

When we first put this idea forward, it was predictably opposed by the customer. The normally calm and composed CFO of S became extremely angry, and almost left the meeting.

"How can the Top Operator Business Plan be carried out without sufficient funding?" he questioned.

We explained, "The goal for S to become a top operator is fantastic, but the plan should be carried out gradually. As an old saying in China goes, 'a mouthful of food won't make you grow fat'. Success doesn't happen overnight. Based on the current revenue and expenses of S, it is our view that the company doesn't need such a large amount of financing over the next two to three years. It would cause great stress and risk to both CDB and Huawei to provide such an enormous amount of financing. It would also affect the stable development of S. It is better to take things gradually and go step by step."

Therefore, half of the financing was cut, a decision that was agreed upon by all three parties after multiple rounds of negotiation. However, removing the 'excess' of the financing proposal was just the beginning of the journey to reach the final cooperation agreement. Many conditions relating to financing still needed to be negotiated and a balance had to be struck between what was required by Huawei and S, respectively.

Many other issues in addition to financing were raised during the negotiations. In the later stages of negotiations, Zhang and other colleagues in the Poland Office prepared a list of remaining issues, with requirements and opinions of each party listed in detail. Zhang discussed the issues with colleagues before each round of negotiation, which helped to make negotiations more effective and efficient. The General Manager of the Poland Office at the time, Gan Jianhua, was also an experienced negotiator. He coordinated negotiations and helped to strike a balance between the interests of all three parties.

After all other issues had been settled, there was still one clause that the two parties couldn't agree on. It was a commonly used clause which stated that S, as the customer, was required to use a certain percentage of the financing to buy equipment for network construction, while the rest could be used for operations. The issue of contention was the percentage of financing that needed to be used for buying the equipment. S wanted a lower percentage so that the money could be used more flexibly.

Neither Huawei nor S was willing to compromise on this issue. The financing manager Zhang, who was normally gentle and composed, became irritated. At certain points in the discussion, he was even becoming too agitated to speak. A CBD lawyer patted him on the shoulder and said, "Don't worry. Conflicts are normal in negotiation. Look at it this way: this shows that all of us are serious about this cooperation."

During one break in negotiations, Zhang lit a cigarette and tried to calm himself down. He organized his thoughts and made the map in his mind clear. Huawei had played a critical role in the previous success of S. If S's business was compared to a spark, then its sound operations could be viewed as the wind, and the high-quality networks provided by Huawei as the fuel that together made the spark shine and grow into a true flame. Huawei's cooperation with S was also an essential factor for CDB to support S. If the customer spent a huge amount of money on its operations and decreased its investment in buying Huawei's equipment to build high-quality networks, would it still be possible for it to develop in a stable manner? Would CBD be paid off in time? Possibly not. It was for these reasons that Huawei chose to maintain its position and refused to compromise.

After several rounds of negotiation, we finally decided upon a percentage that could be accepted by all parties. When the negotiations finished, the CFO of S shook hands with Zhang, saying, "We have been opponents at the negotiating table but I would now consider us close friends."

Flowing into the Sea

Again in the autumn, in October 2011, the three parties signed a third round of financing agreements and contracts, and prepared for new cooperation. As Huawei's regional president Li Jian noted during the signing ceremony, "The additional financing further enhances the strategic cooperation of our three parties, provides sufficient funds for S's continued development, and sets a solid foundation for further cooperation between S and Huawei."

Slowly but surely, S grew and expanded towards maturity. By the end of 2013, S held a market share of more than 15%, and had improved its operations, gradually receiving recognition from the local capital market. In early 2014, S issued corporate bonds through the local capital market and paid off all loans, in one lump sum, in advance.

Although financing is no longer part of the cooperation between Huawei and S, the close relationship built through the financing has been extremely influential on the partnership. S has become the second largest operator in Poland and becoming the top player in the industry no longer seems so far-fetched. The cooperation between Huawei and S has set an example that is encouraging new stories in other countries like Chile, where a new chapter of cooperation is about to be written.

The Vistula River thaws in the spring and the river flows northward through mountains and hills. S was once like the ice and snow on the Beskids Mountains. It was the cooperation with Huawei and CDB that generated the warmth needed to melt the ice and allow the water of the river to make its way to the sea.

How to Sort Out the Books

By Cai Zhijian

Out of all my 10 plus years at Huawei, 2011 was the toughest. I was under so much stress that I even wanted to resign at one point. Back then, I was the CFO of the Southern South American Region. I found that one of our potential sales projects involved a commercial strategy that might expose us to extremely serious legal risks. The project was then escalated to upper management, and finally it was decided that we should not take it on. Suddenly, I was thrust into the middle of controversy. At Huawei, the finance department is usually very much a backroom entity. We generally don't intervene in business operations. But this project in Latin America made all of us realize that we could not blindly go full speed ahead and completely ignore risks. Financial fraud had brought down multinational companies like Enron and WorldCom, and even landed their executives in jail. These scandals reminded Huawei that we must always ensure we comply with all financial laws, and that our risks must be well managed.

In early 2013, the company decided to establish a system of internal controls over financial reporting (ICFR). The purpose was to ensure that our books always accurately reflected the realities of our business, and to bring as much clarity and certainty as we could to the uncertainties we face. I was appointed to manage this project. But the project team was divided on how to build such a system.

The Path to Transformation

For over 10 years, KPMG has given an unqualified opinion on Huawei's financial reports. This indicates that Huawei's financial reports are fairly presented and reliable. This was a hard-won result. At accounting close, nearly 1,000 accountants used to work day and night. We have over 200 subsidiaries, and each has 30 to 50 accounting control points. The accountants had to check them one by one. Every month accountants registered about 40,000 contracts. During the last-minute rush at quarter or year end, our accountants had to check the control points almost every day. When we found any abnormalities because someone on the business side had not followed the rules, we had to check back and forth with the team on the business side to make sure we had properly caught and corrected the error. Sometimes, to adjust a single abnormality, accountants had to go through tens of thousands of entries by hand. There have been cases where our computers crash because we had to use them to trawl through more data than they could handle.

But this old-fashioned manual approach couldn't sustain us forever as Huawei's business grew bigger. The huge volume of adjustments made actually showed that we weren't following procedures very well. In some cases the gaps between our books and reality were actually caused by fraud. So we asked ourselves, how should we establish an effective ICFR system so that our financial reports could truly mirror our business operations?

To better understand the realities of the task ahead of us, we invited consultants from KPMG to carry out a stringent assessment of our existing ICFR.

Early on in the assessment process, one consultant told me, "A dozen experts have read thousands of process documents over the past two weeks, but we still haven't got a clear picture of how financial data flows around Huawei." He pointed out our problem: finance was not aligned with the business side at all. We didn't speak the same language; we didn't talk regularly, or have any mechanisms for working together; and there was no single set of basic data that covered the entire business process, from transactions through to final accounting.

To solve these problems, finance and the business side would have to work together and find a common language so they could ultimately achieve more together than they did separately. This meant that for effective ICFR, finance and business departments needed to be deeply integrated.

The Huawei Group CFO, Sabrina Meng, says, "The objectivity, completeness, and accuracy of data determines the quality of financial reports." This is absolutely right. Finance does not generate data; all financial data comes from the business side. Just as the saying goes, "A river is only as clean as its source." Only when the data coming from upstream is clean can the back-end financial reports be accurate. So to produce high-quality financial reports, we must start with data quality management. This is what we called ICFR.

An Angry Email

For a transformation to succeed, you need to first change people's mindsets. After that you can change their way of doing things. So how were we to establish an awareness of ICFR among Huawei staff?

At the end of 2013, when the business teams were in the middle of their end-of-year push for targets, the Accounting Shared Service Center (SSC) received a complaint from a very angry business manager: "How much of our sales revenue is going to be reversed this year? You always wait until the last day to tell us that this document isn't compliant, or that we never received that payment, so my team's sales revenue has to be rolled back. We triggered revenue recognition for some of these contracts nearly a year ago. You are supposed to be monitoring this stuff. You have to tell us earlier if there's a problem."

This kind of complaint was common. The business staff thought that the finance department should take care of the quality of financial data and that their only job was to get orders and earn more profits. They didn't realize that we could only produce accurate financial data when they provided accurate data and managed their documentation properly.

We shouldn't blame the business teams for their lack of awareness, as there was no policy back then. So the first priority for us was to develop a clean data policy, which we could then implement and enforce. Once we realized that, we issued a series of key regulations and directives.

In July 2014, the Group CFO signed our *Regulations on Internal Controls for Financing Reporting.* This regulation clearly defined the responsibilities of our CEOs, CFOs, and process owners. A set of supporting policies were also developed to ensure that we locked in the new practices.

In August 2014, the Finance Committee issued the *Resolution on Disciplinary Action for Faking Sales Revenue.* It stipulated that anyone who was caught falsifying sales figures would be disciplined for a breach of ethics. This demonstrated that the company was shifting to zero tolerance for massaged sales figures.

In September 2014, the Huawei CFO approved the directive *Signing Letters of Commitment to Internal Controls over Financing Reporting.* 290 CEOs and CFOs, 41 process owners, and 1,032 business managers, signed letters of commitment to the ICFR.

In October 2014, the Huawei Executive Management Team passed the *Resolution on Disciplinary Rules for Business Fraud,* stipulating that anyone who faked their sales results and caused an error in our financial reports would be fired.

This flurry of new regulations clearly showed that the business side had to share the responsibility for accurate financial reporting. But how could we tell if the sales results we saw were indeed clean? This was our next tough issue.

ICFR Proves its Worth

The CFO, Sabrina Meng, had charged us with developing a quantifiable, measurable, and manageable ICFR assessment system.

So what should the key metrics be? Rather than reinventing the wheel, we decided to optimize the existing metrics based on the latest set of problems. Long before we started work on ICFR, the accounting department had many metrics to monitor process compliance, so we could systematize these metrics. We then finalized the key metrics based on the kinds of issues we faced, and started applying them to our business processes.

We selected samples from our past business records, about 1,500 records from each month for each country office, making sure to include all abnormal data that had already been flagged. We applied our new metrics to identify non-compliant data, and compared these transactions against the acceptable error rates set by management. Then we produced a compliance score for each country office and each process. After more than six months of tests and tweaking the system, our ICFR assessment system was ready to go.

The assessment brought improvements to our business. Although we had performed compliance assessments in the past, they were not systematic and weren't linked to any follow-up improvements. Now all offices around the world could use the same dashboard, the same language, and the same criteria to assess their ICFR. This system became an effective tool for improving the way the company works. The process control director of the Global Technical Services Department said ICFR assessments had become a driver of improvements in their operations, and they were much clearer about how well they were doing. IBM consultants marvelled that with this management tool, Huawei's ICFR management was more advanced than many publicly-listed multinationals.

After winning praise both inside and outside the company, it was time to put our ICFR toolset to work. We carried out an assessment of ICFR on all regional offices and departments at the end of 2014, and announced the results publicly within the company for the first time. Two regional offices got 'Very Unsatisfactory' compliance scores. The presidents of these two offices urged their staff to improve, saying, "What are our problems? Please root them out. Ensuring that accounts match business realities is the first and last thing that a business manager must do. If we fail to do even that, then how can we look at ourselves in the mirror? We must do a good job in ICFR. We must fight for our self-respect!" We also published the details of a case of faked sales figures. The general manager of the country office and the managers involved were immediately removed from their positions.

After the ICFR results were announced across the company, the business side was facing some of the pressure that we had to deal with. Compliance did start to improve across the board. But would managers really take responsibility for improving the quality of their data?

Handling the Backlash

In early 2015, the Group Finance Department issued a new regulation which defined CEOs, CFOs, and process owners as those responsible for ensuring accounts match business realities. They would share responsibility for the quality of our financial reports by carrying out their duties, identifying problems, finding solutions, and making improvements.

ICFR was soon deployed across the whole company. All regional offices began revisiting historical problems, controlling new issues, reviewing their business processes, integrating solutions, training staff members, and adjusting their organization structure. Very quickly, the frontline staff started to feel the stress of ensuring high quality data. ICFR was affecting how they worked in a way we had never done before. With swift, effective changes, some major issues relating to ICFR were quickly resolved.

However, this process was surely a challenge to some of Huawei's old ways of thinking and handling business. Along the way, some of the ICFR tools got a little twisted, and that raised some dissenting voices.

One incident was so serious that it was written up and published to the whole Huawei group: a regional office had asked a customer to repeatedly sign and apply its seal until the customer got fed up. On Huawei's internal discussion forum, a number of people criticized ICFR. They thought that ICFR had gone too far. They thought it was now a hindrance to the company's operations and was even causing us to lose business.

Du Yanxin, the owner of the ICFR project, worked with his team members, leading a series of discussions and reflections on the current problems. Following that, everyone was on the same page: the new ICFR was broadly correct. Its benefits and value had been shown, and we must continue on with it. The transformation had now entered a much more intractable phase, where it was triggering conflict with past practices. If we didn't do something, we would surely fail. Actually it wasn't a bad thing that ICFR was running into resistance. It was an opportunity for us to improve on our work. Du told the project team to visit field offices, listen to what the local teams were saying, and think about how to make systematic improvements.

Group CFO Sabrina Meng emphasized again, "Ensuring accounts match business realities is the foundation for credible financial reporting. Enforcing an ownership system for ICFR is standard practice throughout our industry." Her message helped to strengthen our resolve.

So the project team then improved the rules for measuring and assessing ICFR and guided the regions on how to build their long-term systems for ICFR. They also further empowered regional CFOs, to make sure that the people closest to the action were the ones making the decisions.

These measures helped create a better environment for ICFR. However, to help the business side truly understand the importance of ICFR, external pressure would never be enough. They would only recognize the value of ICFR when they saw the benefits for themselves.

You Reap What You Sow

One Huawei office in country M was attracting attention from the local media because it was late making a payment to a supplier. The issue was damaging Huawei's reputation and made it difficult for us to win contracts in the local market. The reason for the delay was that the payment process in the local office was not efficient. In fact 70% of payments to suppliers were delayed. Before the media attention began, accounting staff had spotted the problems with the office's payables, and had reminded the office to fix the problems several times. But the office didn't pay enough attention to the issue. The supplier couldn't get paid after finishing their work, and the accounts payable were sitting on Huawei's books for much longer than they were supposed to. It was a mismatch between the financial accounts and business actuals: a classic ICFR issue.

The local ICFR project team had an in-depth discussion with the teams on the ground in country M to try to jointly find a solution. In the end, the local office decided to take several actions. First, they improved their processes to make the end-to-end process more visible and manageable. Second, they increased expertise in the local team and provided extra training to local staff. Third, they phased out 342 small suppliers and expanded their links with 45 strategic suppliers. Fourth, they managed contract payment terms and improved fulfillment quality. The local office soon turned the situation around. Less than 3% of payments were delayed. The general manager no longer needed to worry about payments and could focus on how to better serve customers. The office also saw a sharp rise in its ICFR score.

In another country, a project manager named Lai arrived to take over an old project in July 2015. The project was a total mess. The office had a revenue target for that year of CNY112 million, but by July they had only managed to make 30% of that. Inventory was piled up in the warehouse; costs amounting to over CNY30 million had not been properly rolled over in the accounts; inventory was held over 200 days before being sold; about 800 invoices were rejected each month; and customer complaints were flooding in. All of the actual work for the customer had been finished long ago, but because the accounts had not been done correctly, we couldn't even collect payment from the customer. The project's ICFR assessment score was very poor.

Lai used the ICFR assessment as a guide to work out what the issues were. Quickly Lai found that the real problem was a mismatch between the customer's processes and Huawei's processes.

The project team quickly made improvements, linking up Huawei's processes for handing over a completed piece of work, and the customer's processes for inspecting and accepting it. Once the two companies' IT systems were able to talk to each other, the problems were solved. The amount of inventory piled up in the warehouse was reduced from CNY28 million to CNY2 million; long overdue inventory fell by 62%. We were able to recognize revenue at three times the previous rate. By the end of 2015, the project team had exceeded its revenue target and rather than getting complaints, we received several letters of appreciation from the customer.

Forging Ahead

Since 2016, we have seen more success stories where ICFR has helped drive improvements on the business side. These stories have been widely shared within the company, and more managers have started to embrace ICFR.

The delivery manager in the Indonesia Office said, "In 2015, we started to work on uncollected receivables and clearing up inventory. The results are tangible: we brought in US$11 million of revenue and cleared out inventory worth US$4.4 million. That means we had an additional US$7 million in our pockets! We also streamlined our processes. Now, after a base station passes its acceptance inspections, project revenue can be recognized immediately. In the past, we had to work through the night confirming all the figures with the accounting staff, and there were always so many arguments! Now our plans are much more accurate, and everyone knows what they are doing."

The procurement manager of the South Pacific Region said, "The ICFR project has helped us streamline our processes and shorten our turnaround time. Our suppliers can get paid immediately after their work is accepted, so they are more willing to work with Huawei and provide us with their best services."

In August 2016, the Huawei Internal Audit Department assessed the risk controls on the Huawei Group's sales revenue. For the first time, it gave a rating of 'Satisfactory'. There has been a sharp decline in high-risk revenue which cannot be collected within the current year. We've achieved the best level in Huawei's history.

At the end of 2016, the quality of Huawei's ICFR reached the 'Basically Satisfactory' level. We have good controls over false reporting of revenue; the number of accounts that have to be adjusted has declined by 50%; compliance in our payment processes has improved dramatically; and some metrics for payment accuracy are now as good as any company in our industry.

Our external auditor said that Huawei's accounting and internal controls are continuously improving; our financial reporting is higher quality; variances and adjustments identified during audit continue to decline; and significant improvements have been made in revenues and costs. Today only 0.019% of these items need adjusting after the fact.

However, we are well aware that we still have a long way to go. How can ICFR better support the business we do in our local offices? How can we make sure that our financial reports are accurate and fair reflections of our business, and at the same time make the ICFR checks a sustainable part of our processes? How can we produce satisfactory financial reports? These are the challenges that we need to work harder on.

13

How the Dashboard Came to Be

By Liu Jianhua

As Huawei approaches its 30th year, its footprint extends to over 170 countries and regions. But how could we steer this huge vessel without a dashboard capable of giving us an instant and accurate snapshot of the company's operations?

I Receive My Orders, R&A Sets Sail

Huawei set up systems for financial reporting back in 2003, but we didn't have the proper architecture. Over the years, more than 2,000 patches have been applied to the IT system. This disorganized approach resulted in slow and clumsy accounting procedures. Every accounting close, our finance team had to work around the clock to get the books in good order. Finance staff working in local offices had to collect financial data and fill out financial reports by hand. Monthly operation reviews for business units were often delayed by two weeks, or even a whole month. When the figures were finally presented, they were already so dated that we used to call those meetings 'memorial services'. Another problem was related to the logic behind the figures. If a department questioned the accounts, the finance team themselves were often unable to explain how they had finally calculated these numbers. Accounting and reporting had become a major problem for the finance department.

In 2005, Huawei's finance management team went to IBM's headquarters on a study tour and was stunned by IBM's reporting and analysis system. Sabrina Meng, the company's CFO, recalled that it was after that trip that she made up her mind to make reporting and analysis (R&A) a key part of the broader Integrated Financial Services (IFS) transformation program. We were running this program to improve our finance systems.

After some initial experiments and research, the project team and our consultants concluded: to create a dashboard like IBM's, Huawei must first set up an effective system for accounting and reporting. However, the truth was that our accounting and reporting team had been overwhelmed by the rapid growth of our business. In order to be effective in the long term, our existing systems would have to be abandoned and replaced by completely new architecture.

Accounting and reporting is the foundation of finance. Replacing the old system with a completely new one is like trying to swap out the engine of a car as it speeds along the highway. It would take a huge injection of human resources and capital, and there was considerable risk. According to a rough analysis by our IBM consultants, it would cost hundreds of millions of RMB and take at least three years to restructure our systems, given the large size and complexity of Huawei.

The finance leadership was still determined to carry out the transformation. They sent out the order: find the resources and secure the budget needed to transform our reporting and analysis practices. Huawei needs a new financial accounting and reporting platform!

In late 2009, the R&A project got fully under way. The team pulled in experts on accounting solutions from finance, operations, and the business process and IT departments. In addition, some business managers from overseas offices were brought in to help us talk to the business side and understand their needs. Back then, I was in charge of finance for the European region, and I was fortunate enough to be recruited to the project team.

Difficulties Finding the Right Way Forward

It was an all-star lineup: one VP, seven directors, 10 senior experts from IBM, and over 50 project team members, all of them senior experts in their own right.

But making progress proved extremely difficult. Accounting affects every area of the company's business, so every little change we made had a direct impact upon somebody's job. And every department had its own understandings and demands.

The large size and complexity of the company means that we have to handle many different accounting rules. We also have to meet demands from different business domains and different levels of the company.

Another problem was linked with setting priorities. We had taken accounting experts from many departments, so we often got side-tracked by their emergency requests for help or when they had problems with their long-term solutions. We were stuck, being pulled in a dozen directions at once. Three months after I joined the team, I was made the fourth project manager for R&A. Frequent changes in leadership had left team morale low, and the whole team was struggling to find a way forward.

Should we turn left, or turn right?

Financial data comes from the business side. But the transaction systems we developed in the early years of Huawei were not well planned out, and financial data was scattered everywhere. So, when the data finally flowed to the backend, i.e. the accounting department, we often had to clean, translate, or even reconstruct the numbers.

The large size and complexity of the company means that we have to handle many different accounting rules. We also have to meet demands from different business domains and different levels of the company. Now we were going to ask our people to do accounting from more dimensions, and to be far more granular. That would require a high level of accounting expertise.

Should we first tackle the problems with source data, or first try to build up our accounting skills? After taking a closer look at the problem, the project team realized that source data had extensive impacts on the quality of financial data. However, we wouldn't be able to fix the problems with the source data until we could express exactly what they were. Therefore, the first thing to do was build up our own expertise in accounting and reporting, figure out how the data was being handled, and improve our ability to monitor data quality. This would help us to improve the quality of the data flowing from the business side.

The new project leader, Li Hua, came to join our debate, and he strongly endorsed our focus on building up our own expertise first. This finally solved our classic chicken-and-egg dilemma.

Solution Design Is an Incremental Process

Once a consensus was reached, we began working on the design of our new system. What kind of accounting and reporting system would support our goals without the need to be frequently changed, given the many complex and evolving accounting rules? It felt like trying to teach an elephant ballet: virtually mission impossible. But we had to get started, so we followed our consultants' recommendation to divide the project team into four sub-groups to tackle different aspects of the issue.

The accounting rules group. Every core member was a born accountant: Mao Zhi was careful and well-organized; Lu Zhen was a walking dictionary of accountancy, who knew the chapter and verse of every accounting code; and Jiang Feng was our quick-witted man of action. To build an accounting platform, the first step was to make all of the accounting rules clear. Accounting rules link directly to the company's priorities and the interests of individual departments, so it took the team more than a year to negotiate exactly what the rules were with each separate department. But finally, we had a buy-in from everyone and a complete set of accounting rules. Just to give you an example, when they were drafting the plan for a 'responsibility centre', the plan had to go to the Finance Committee for approval three times, and to the Executive Management Team twice before it was finally agreed. Every aspect of the document had to be utterly watertight. Along the way, the accounting rules team carried out a comprehensive analysis of IBM's practices. Even our IBM consultants were impressed – they said they had never seen such a thorough analysis before. So on this occasion the 'teachers' learned something from their 'students'!

The report design group. When the accounting process is complete, how do we present the financial data to our users? How do we use it to identify problems in our business management and support our decisions? These were the questions for the second group. Zhai Yonghui was the team leader. He did not have experience with finance, but had many years of experience working directly with customers at the Global Technical Services. He knew exactly what customers wanted. He worked with two finance experts, Liu Mo and Li Guixu, to examine various customer needs. Eventually, they concluded that there were essentially two types of financial reports: (1) Standard reports that provide official information about the company. This type includes more than 2,000 reports in eight categories, for different financial subjects and business domains; (2) Customized reports based on user-defined criteria, which could be used for internal routine business analyses and decision-making.

The reporting solutions group. This team included many of our sharpest minds on accounting solutions. Jin Yuhong, a senior accounting manager known for her experience and quick thinking, was the team leader. She had two promising young men, Chen Jinshui and Hu Dongliang, as her deputies. This group was responsible for designing all accounting solutions. The job was very demanding, as they had to give precise definitions for each account item and each dimension. The smallest error in a definition could cause wildly misleading figures. With the help of consultants, they developed a way to process financial data on a rolling basis, like an assembly line. It was a pioneering idea, which we called management and consolidated accounting (MCA), and it made possible an accounting system which was structured, modular, and freely configurable. With MCA, thousands of data processing procedures were consolidated into 13 data modules which could be repeatedly applied. This made the generation of financial data much more consistent, replicable, transparent, and traceable. Now that we had this modular approach to accounting rules, we could reflect changes to the company policy in the accounting process by simply reconfiguring a few parameters. Thus our system became much more responsive, and cheaper to maintain.

The IT group. They were involved in every part of the project from the very beginning. They had to be, because this work, which was completely outside-the-box, meant that IT system development was far more difficult than usual.

The group gradually pulled together one idea after another, slowly letting the system evolve, until they achieved a complete working model in late 2011.

Presenting R&A solutions – an international effort

If You Want Something Done Right, Do It Yourself

We took the parameters for our dashboard to several of the world's leading software vendors, and asked what they could do for us. They said that they had never seen anything so complex and large, with such narrow margins for error. All of them said, "Our software can't do that, and there's not much chance that it will be able to anytime soon."

So we had no choice but to develop the software ourselves. We thought, in for a penny, in for a pound, and we set ourselves a tough deadline: we would launch in one year.

Frankly, we had let ourselves get a little carried away. In those days, the business intelligence that we would need simply had not yet been widely applied. Plus, with little expertise in this area, we had no idea about how many development staff we would need.

But we had set the schedule now, so off we started. We didn't have anything to work with at first: no technology, no resources. And our recklessness soon got its come-uppance. The launch of the first release was delayed two months, and when it did arrive, it would not produce any reports. At the year-end wrap-up meeting, one colleague said, "I've seen disorganized projects before, but nothing like this..."

As the project team struggled to make progress, CFO Sabrina Meng stepped in to help. She poached a guy named Lao Wei, one of the top systems architects from the application and software product line. To build a pool of talent, the project team asked Lao to train four team members. We arranged a dinner at which the four pledged to study under Lao like an old kung fu sensei. Those who joined the team later also went through the same process, and in the end everyone came to know Lao Wei as 'Master Lao'. Lao had extensive experience in designing and developing big pieces of software. His expertise was exactly what the project badly needed, and he became a pillar of the whole project.

The business process and IT department also began to prioritize this project. Zhang Yinchen, responsible for the IT part of the whole IFS program, led the implementation of the R&A project in person. Zhang spearheaded many large IT projects like the rollout of ERP and development of Opportunity to Cash (OTC). Under his leadership, many tech-savvy specialists joined the development team. The team grew from a few dozen people to nearly 500 almost overnight. They included Si Xiaokang, Zhang Xingrui, Xiong Dahong, Zhang Mingshi, and Chen Xi.

By late 2012, the building we worked in could no longer accommodate our large team. So the project team was relocated to an empty space on the third floor of a manufacturing base in another section. It was quite a spectacle watching hundreds of people working in such a big room. In the last phase of system development, we were running simulated stress tests. All project members were asked to operate the system at the same time to simulate peak traffic. But the factory was so large that we couldn't hear the instructions. Fortunately, our quick-witted secretary found a loudspeaker from somewhere. Now, when the testing leader Luo Limei gave her loud instructions through the speaker,

The loudspeaker in our software workshop

everybody followed and busied themselves logging on and clicking the dashboard... "I can't log in." "Mine's stuck, too!" "It works! It works!"... The instructions from the loudspeaker mixed with the high and low voices reporting progress. Those nights bustled with noise and excitement.

Speaking of stress tests, there's a story I must tell: determination with a moustache. There is a famous story about Mei Lanfang, the Chinese opera singer, who grew out his beard to show his patriotism. Now Liu Tanren did the same thing, but for a different reason. Liu Tanren was the leader of the platform technology team. As the performance issues persisted, he was so worried that he promised the team at a mobilization meeting that he would not shave until the problems were solved.

The changing shape of Liu Jianhua's moustache

Someone recorded his progress over the final, critical phase of the project. The results were impressive: in the end it took less than 15 seconds to open 90% of the standard, frequently used reports. 72% of the detailed reports could be downloaded in three minutes; 70% of data could be traced within 30 seconds. The overall performance was up by 50%. Liu had lived up to his words.

Over the course of more than one year, the platform development team scored many firsts in the IT history of Huawei. They produced 40,000-page design documents, and performed 24,000 scheduling tasks. Two of our technologies were so new that we were able to obtain two patents in China.

The Launch: 48 Hours That Decided Our Fate

After three years of hard work by so many people, the dashboard was finally approaching its big moment. The project team gave it the name 'iSee'.

We decided to launch iSee on 22 March, 2013. It would be the largest financial system cutover in Huawei's history. When the new system was in place, all financial data would be coming from this single source. If any errors occurred during the cutover, the company would have no financial reports. Failure was not an option.

To ensure a successful cutover, the project team voluntarily worked through the New Year and Chinese Spring Festival holidays. They carried out intensive testing on system functions and performance, drawing in more than 2,800 finance staff and over 40,000 use cases.

At 10am, the project team had to make one last important decision before the cutover: retune the master data or not? The master data had already been fed into the system during system initialization, but then some junk data was generated for some reason. Some colleagues held that it would take too long to clear and retune the master data, not to mention the uncertainty involved. They suggested a partial retuning of the data that had been altered. Others insisted that the data must be cleaned, and that we could only use retuned data for the accounting close and reporting. Otherwise, the whole database would be contaminated by the junk data, which would compromise the operation of the system in the long term. It would be too late to clean the data when the system had been running for a while. This would be both costly and ineffective.

Neither side was backing down in this argument, making the workshop quite a lively place. I told everyone to calm down, and asked several technical experts to check the scheduling function of the system, which proved to be reliable. To play it safe, we could make a backup of the data so that we could return to the original plan in case of failure. Eventually, the project team decided to retune the data to give iSee a fresh and perfect start. This would be our reward for four years of hard work.

At 8pm, staff at our shared service centres began to submit data. When all the data for accounting close was submitted, it was already midnight. And when all transaction data was uploaded, it was 4:30am. Master data retuning continued until 3pm. The data verification results showed that it was a very successful run and that the output data was high quality. The last step was group accounting close, where the powerful data processing 'assembly line' came into play. As datasets were generated by category, staff on the business side immediately began verification.

On 24 March, 7am, all the data was uploaded to the system. The system launch had been a complete success!

Digital Transformation Extends

The launch of iSee marked a new chapter for Huawei's finance operations. Now we could turn on the dashboard at any time to check the company's real-time financial performance, just like IBM.

With the new accounting platform, the finance team's capacity grew. As a result, the turnaround time for the full consolidated reports of the Huawei Group was cut from six days to five. Additionally, the time required to adapt to new accounting requirements was cut from five months to one. We were also now able to analyse and trace the quality of our front-end source data.

After iSee went live, the R&A team was kept together to maintain the platform. In the years that followed, the project team input more basic data into the system, and kept applying new data analytics and data mining tools to use the data more efficiently. In 2015, we used big data analytics for the first time to forecast the group's mid- to long-term cash flow. The accuracy of our forecasts was 95%.

Though it has been four to five years since the R&A transformation, I still remember those days with a sense of excitement. Many project team members said this project was more than just another job. It was a rite of passage where we were able to hone our professional skills, and more importantly, to focus our willpower and learn more about our character.

Personally, the project was a baptism that transformed me from a financial manager to a leader of complex business transformations and IT development. It taught me how to look beyond technology and business operations, and to aim for the ultimate goal: to manage and use people in a smart, open way and to transform a group of specialists into a cohesive team that could work as one to achieve the visions of our company.

The R&A project was the fire, and we – and Huawei – were the phoenixes born again from its ashes!

Days of passionate commitment

It All Started with a Single Penny

By Vickie Chen

My understanding of accounting began with a single penny.

In 2009, I arrived in Argentina, the first stop on my overseas work journey. Upon seeing me so full of enthusiasm and yet so utterly lacking in basic knowledge, my boss just shook his head. "There is an invoice on the ERP system where the customer payment was one cent less than the receipt amount. What do you think should be done?"

I didn't have a clue how to answer that question. My boss gave a hint: I should look to see if the situation met the criteria for small amount adjustment. After investigating, I found that the issue was that the customer had underpaid by one cent. This was the final payment under the contract, so it was possible to make an adjustment. It took me a good half hour to figure out how to make the one cent adjustment in the system. I had to create a virtual receipt, accrue it in non-operating expenses, and submit it to my manager for approval.

I was pushed to my wits' end all for a single penny. My manager told me very seriously: "This isn't about being picky; it is about being strict. If we don't follow the process, then problems could crop up in accounting logic, or there could be compliance issues internally. Small mistakes can lead to big consequences!"

I just nodded enthusiastically. But it really took more than eight years for me to truly understand the meaning of his words.

Developing Intuition About the Numbers

As the new year was rung in on 1 January, 2010, I became involved in my first round of year-end accounting close.

As I stepped into the 'operations room', I saw accountants everywhere hunched over their computer screens. Each was dealing with pre-prepared accounting close plans and was in their own little world as they worked. Accounts receivable accountants would first input the information of invoices and payments from customers, and apply payments to invoices. Then accounts payable accountants would complete supplier payments and straighten out the accounts. Data would be finalized for things like revenue, cost, inventory, and fixed assets. This information would be forwarded to the general ledger department who would generate financial reports. Each step had to be completed before the pre-defined time. As I looked at everyone's furrowed brows, I couldn't help but feel nervous myself. It was like seeing a line of runners waiting for the starting gun to sound. Everyone was gunning for gold, and determined to deliver outstanding results.

I was responsible for revenue and cost accounting for country C. We had two subsidiaries in the country, and two sets of accounts. Data sources involved a dozen or so new and old systems, and much of the work had to be done manually. The work continued right up to nearly midnight. We were struggling to balance the accounts for service costs. We couldn't close the accounts if we didn't find where the variance was. After an entire day of intense effort, I was already at my wits' end. I simply couldn't figure out where the variance was coming from. I was on the verge of a breakdown.

I looked over and over the transactions that I had processed, and simply couldn't find anything wrong with them. The clock was ticking. We had already delayed the general ledger by an hour, and the team over there was pressing us to get things rolling. What could we do? Tears of desperation began to stream down my face as I looked for the problem.

My manager came over. His first words were to tell me to relax. Then he showed me a new way to uncover variances that involved checking the data from a variety of perspectives. I took a deep breath to calm myself, then followed his approach. This finally allowed me to find the culprit in an inconspicuous corner of the numbers. The Excel macro wasn't able to read non-standard contract formatting, and had therefore missed one line of contract data. After it was identified, we could deal with the issue, easy-peasy.

I came to realize that when I got really worked up and anxious, I would make mistakes more easily. Even though my colleagues were working at a slower pace, they very rarely made a mistake. They would constantly console me by saying "take it easy." By learning from their example, I eventually was able to keep a calmer focus on my work. I constantly trained myself to get the numbers done right the first time. Even though I was just one cog in a large accounting machine, the entire contraption could be brought to a halt if I made a mistake. The veracity, accuracy, and timeliness of the company's financial reports could be seriously affected by any error. With such a solemn mission, we couldn't allow ourselves to overlook even the smallest detail.

Of course, there is joy to be found when exploring the world of numbers that is accounting. Over the course of several years, I developed an intuition for the numbers. I moved from being lost in a veritable forest of numbers in the Excel spreadsheets, to being able to quickly find key data logic as well as errors across multiple spreadsheets.

Disentangling a US$50 Million Knot

In 2011, I was responsible for accounts receivable work at the Mexico and Central America Offices. One day, I received a request from a finance manager in Jamaica. Operator A was being acquired. Huawei had a long overdue receivable for civil works totaling US$50 million with the operator. The amount had not yet been paid.

I quickly made arrangements to visit the office in Jamaica. The contract for the project in question had been signed in 2007. But after acceptance in 2009, the customer had claimed that the network had failed to meet the stated requirements. Based on this claim, the customer had not made the payment upon acceptance as per contract requirements. "Is there anything you can do to help?" The finance manager's face revealed how concerned he was.

The project was already four years old, and many of its documents had been misplaced. It wouldn't be an easy task to go back to the technical departments of both parties and get replacement documents. I had to visit the customer's offices every day and work with their accounts payable staff on the reconciliations. But I never imagined that a month into the work, the customer's CFO would ask that Huawei first sign off on the balance payable recorded in the system before continuing with the review. They claimed this request was for internal requirements. The issue was that there was a variance of many tens of millions of US dollars between the balance payable recorded by Huawei and the record of the customer. This was precisely the source of the disagreement between the parties, so our finance manager naturally couldn't agree to such a request. The customer's CFO ordered that the reconciliation work be put on hold.

Were we really going to give up, just like that? Every penny involved was potential profit for the company! After giving the issue a lot of thought, I realized something. The customer's CTO had a straightforward personality and was a friendly fellow. The deeper reason for not paying was a delivery dispute. So we asked the CTO to help convince the CFO to continue the reconciliation efforts.

"What about if you first clarify the costs for every base station?" The CTO asked this direct question, then continued to explain: "I am not trying to cause trouble. I mention this because we issue purchase orders (POs) and carry out acceptance inspections by base station. Invoices are issued by base station, but your company hasn't yet issued the invoices. This is why we're looking at such a mess."

After hearing the honest feedback from the customer, I knew that what needed to be done was to link up invoices to their corresponding base stations. So I made a bold commitment: "Even if the records between our two parties are as knotted and disorganized as a ball of string, I will find a way to sort it all out!"

Having made the big commitment, the only thing to do then was to press onward to live up to my promise. The project amount exceeded US$100 million, but only the amounts of a few larger contracts were shown in the system. In reality, each of those contracts represented over a hundred different POs. More worrying still, Huawei's systems were generating corresponding statements based on internal contract numbers and invoice serial numbers. On customer payment vouchers, all that was displayed were a tax invoice number and PO number. The identifiers on paperwork between Huawei and the customer were completely different, making it very difficult to connect up the paperwork from the two sides. The further back in time one looked, the more complex it became to match up information.

To untie this 'knot' would require manual preparation of reconciliation statements. POs were issued by base station, which meant we had to start from the PO numbers. One PO number corresponded to one base station. There was a Preliminary Acceptance Certificate (PAC) and a Final Acceptance Certificate (FAC). The PO and these two certificates could be matched up to an invoice for prepayment, an invoice for preliminary acceptance payment, and an invoice for final acceptance payment. This was all the information we needed to get the books in proper order.

Reconciliation wasn't something we could do all on our own. We needed the participation of the customer. To this end, each day we made a point of sticking around the customer's offices. We sorted through one dusty box after another alongside their accounts payable accountants, looking for the required documents amidst the aging piles of papers. I was really moved by the fact that the customer's finance staff would on many occasions work overtime deep into the night with me, simply because they themselves were inspired by the conscientiousness of Huawei's team.

Lying in my bed each night, all I would think about was what I had to do next to get the job done. My dreams were filled with data to be organized. As the books became better organized, we gradually got a better picture of the project. In order to accelerate progress in reconciliation work, I took the approach of first clearing the easier accounts. I broke the reconciliation work down into three large categories: devices, equipment, and civil works.

I decided to have the customer first sign-off on the statements for devices and equipment, then deal with the tougher activity involving civil works.

The reconciliation work was completed over the course of three months. The invoices issued by base station were each matched up correctly, which left the customer's CFO fully satisfied. He told me, somewhat apologetically: "You sure are a persistent one. Nice work!" One week later, the customer made a payment for US$50 million.

From Being Separated by an Unfathomable Distance, to Standing Side-by-side

Of course, in addition to working with our customers, we in finance also have to work with our own business departments.

In 2012, we noticed that the revenue of the Colombia Office was being adjusted frequently. There were serious issues related to low inventory turnover, and there were always applications at month-end for account adjustments. My boss sent me to investigate, review the books, and figure out how to make improvements.

When I arrived at the office, I sent one e-mail after another to their business departments, asking all sorts of things and looking for ways to make positive changes. But the delivery manager didn't give me the time of day. At the time, it was my opinion that business staff were just looking out for their own interests. They were not following procedures when using the system, which meant that a lot of work had to be done later on by finance to pick up the pieces. So I eventually changed to a sharper tone and asked during a meeting: "After the processes developed by the Integrated Financial Services (IFS)[3] program were deployed, why have you still been making so many account adjustments and causing

3 Integrated Financial Services (IFS) is a transformation undertaken by Huawei to improve finance operations.

189

so many headaches for finance to sort out?" The sharp words made for an uncomfortable atmosphere in the meeting room.

But the answer from the delivery manager caught me off guard: "We are supportive of the transformation, but the reality of business makes it hard for us to immediately and completely comply with the global standardized process. You can't take a one-size-fits-all approach. There has to be a gradual process of change to achieve improvement."

That got me thinking. The business team did have a point. Rather than just talk about it, it would be better for us to get more involved in projects and provide more feasible and constructive suggestions for improvement. With these thoughts in mind, early the next day I went with the project team to a base station to learn more about the conditions on the ground.

"What's this?"

"It's the DBS 3900."[4] The project manager opened the machine cabinet and let me have a look inside.

"What's that pointy thing at the top of the tower?"

"It's a distributed base station." I also went to the warehouse for an inventory and saw many products in person, and got a better understanding of their shapes and sizes. All of those codes in the bills of materials (BOMs) that I had so often seen in Excel spreadsheets were suddenly materializing right before my eyes, true to life. As I looked at each, I would be estimating the cost of each of them in turn.

After a few days, I had gained a reasonable understanding of the project and could begin speaking on more level terms with the delivery manager, as well as people in charge of logistics, invoicing, and IT.

"Why are there over 100 base stations with which we have recorded costs, but only a dozen in the quote? Revenue is broken

4 DBS 3900 is a model of a distributed base station developed by Huawei and widely deployed around the world.

down by the number of base stations in the quote, whereas cost is based on the actual number of base stations. This will cause a serious variance between the revenue and cost of each base station. Why does the local office's goods demand plan go faster than the delivery progress? How about we have a careful look at the contract to see if there was room for improvement when it was signed?" As a finance employee, I gave my opinion from an expert perspective. I laid out a long series of issues, things they had never thought about before. As they heard my questions, they suddenly realized that they might have been managing things too loosely in the past and needed to improve.

With each question and corresponding answer, the business teams became more and more willing to accept my opinions. Beginning at that time, they also realized that by not following processes, they were causing a lot of extra work for back-end staff.

Over the course of that year, I went over the entire process with the project manager. We carefully studied business activities connected to revenue and cost data entry, and listed out common problems. Then we sat down with business managers, and those discussions were often heated, to say the least. But even the most noticeable bruise does eventually fade. The delivery manager laughed, "I never imaged that business could be handled so smoothly by following the processes established by IFS!"

The former seemingly unfathomable gap between us, and the ensuing arguments, had been resolved. By talking about the issues in person, past grudges were forgotten. Revenue processes were streamlined, enabling more self-directed management by the Project Management Office (PMO).

As the year of support was coming to an end, a delivery colleague called me out of the blue: "I've got an urgent matter. Get over here quick." I ran all the way up to the office on the 15th floor, only to find a huge box of snacks and a beautiful bouquet of flowers awaiting me. They said to me sincerely that they wanted to work overtime alongside me to learn about the accounting close process. In that moment, I couldn't have been happier.

Having Your Books in Order Is the Only Way to Be an Outstanding Manager

So was there any way to get even closer to business? Yes! In 2013, I gave myself a new challenge. I worked as a project financial controller (PFC) at the Ecuador Office.

I definitely had my hands full with the new position, and problems rained down like volcanic ash from an erupting volcano. I first led three employees in deploying the Project Financial Management (PFM) system in the country. It took us half a year to iron out all the issues with systems and processes. The finances of the country's civil works projects were where the biggest headaches existed. These involved long delivery cycles, and there were a wide range of complex processes touching on-site survey, digging, cable-laying, tower-building, and road construction. We were also hiring many local employees. Before the PFM switchover, the project had been running for three years. The new system wasn't able to display the detailed cost data from before the switchover.

I thought about the issue for a bit, and realized we had to have the ledger in order if we wanted to have a clear view of transactions of the project. But this was definitely easier said than done. If we didn't do it right, the issue could come back to bite us later. The project amount was US$120 million. Data was disorganized, and strewn across the minds and computers of countless colleagues. To get the ledger in order, I had to ask for data from other colleagues, and also search knowledge bases. I even had to glean information from external websites. Because of changes in scenarios and management requirements, this data couldn't just be directly used once obtained. We had to analyse, process, and refine the data. Because of this, I often found myself having to 'run into' people in the office, so that I could learn the real drivers behind the project activities from the PMO and project managers.

It was often frustrating work when things all came to a head. Data sources of project costs were just so complex, and there were way too many sub-scenarios. I came close to just giving up.

After all, this wasn't exactly a fixed KPI for me, right? I could just let it slide. But I cut my train of thought short as soon as such ideas began to float around my mind. If I couldn't even sort out the books, then managing the project as a whole was simply out of the question. If we didn't get this sorted out, then how could I speak on a level footing with a highly experienced project manager? Finally, the perfectionist inside me won out over complacency.

Six months later, I made the most complete and detailed book in the history of the office. There were summaries, all sorts of details, and everything else one could possibly imagine. The book provided quantifiable records for transactions, major events, and risks. It provided an important reference for the project team. Even newcomers to the project could quickly come to understand the project by referring to the information I put together.

However, it wasn't enough just to provide data. By analyzing the financial data, I discovered that the project team's labour costs were high, and that the service items were recording monthly losses. After confirming the situation with the project team, I recommended that the deputy general manager in charge of delivery make needed adjustments to the utilization of labour. This achieved a reduction of US$50,000 in costs the same month. Later on, every time the office staff discussed sales opportunities and had finance-related questions, the CFO would call me in.

Uncovering the Actual Needs of Customers

In addition to participating in the project delivery process, I also hoped to be involved in the financial solution design before contract signing. In 2016, I had the opportunity to oversee ongoing projects of the Key Project Department.

The first team to call me in was the Network Sales Solutions Department in one of the company's account departments. A customer had decided to modernize its fixed network in the country. The project entailed massive investment and long-term planning. Civil works accounted for a large proportion of the project.

Normally, a customer financing approach would have been taken, but the customer was insisting on not borrowing money. They were not willing to finance the project.

I discussed customer investment with the project team, and interpreted the customer's financial reports in collaboration with the account department's finance staff. Together, we discovered that the customer looked at the longer term regarding finances. The customer was very determined to build its network, so why was it taking so long to give the project a budget? Digging further into its financial problems, we were able to find the actual reason: they were short on cash. So behind the refusal to borrow money was the fact that this customer was worried about the burden that could be caused by becoming asset-heavy.

The next thing to figure out was whether we could find a business model that could resolve the cash issue while also allowing the company to operate in an asset-light manner. Changes to the accounting treatment of leases in the International Accounting Standards (IAS) made it much harder to operate in an asset-light model. A week passed. The deadline set for response to the customer was approaching, and we still hadn't come up with a satisfactory business model.

I was really concerned, and I spent my days with a furrowed brow and a gloomy demeanour as I contemplated the issue. Then one day, I happened to run into an old friend of mine at the company. I told him about the trouble I was having, and was surprised to hear him mention an interesting concept. He was talking about two or more telecom operators using the same basic network. For telecom operators, this could greatly reduce basic network investment costs. Some of their assets could thereby be taken off the books by finding a third party to oversee heavy assets. Yes, that was it! The idea of 'sharing' was like a light in the darkness for me. It showed me a glimmer of hope.

Next, I sought out further information from customer financing colleagues and poured through all of the business model and financial materials once again. I read through that information like I was counting jewels and pearls. Once I wrapped my head around that information, I went to speak with finance colleagues in the account department to map out a model diagram.

We were fortunate enough to have our plan accepted by the regional finance department as well as the account department's finance team. The customer eventually agreed to utilize a mixed method of using the traditional approach to network construction while plotting out an area for trial use of the new business model. The project is still ongoing, but has thus far seen some success. This was the first time I stood at the forefront of the Lead to Cash (LTC) process, blazing the trail alongside frontline teams.

Looking back on the past eight years, it really did all start with a single penny. My work later progressed toward projects worth over a hundred million US dollars, and I have been involved in accounting at the backend as well as finances at the front end. I will always remember what my manager said to me: "Treat every cent seriously." Be meticulous, be patient, and be responsible. Do everything to the best of your ability.

Eight years really isn't all that long. I will continue my journey, rolling up my sleeves to get the job done, and done right.

The Most Accurate Accurate Financial Reports Possible

By Shi Yanli

My decision to join Huawei was an act of rebellion.

When I was young, I generally did exactly what was expected of me. So when I went to college, I chose the major that my parents wanted me to study. When I finished my master's degree, my parents wanted me to do more postgrad work and ultimately become a university lecturer or a civil servant. But I was done with schooling. When the Huawei recruitment team came to my university, I seized the opportunity and signed up with the company there and then. It was the biggest decision I had ever made for myself.

I had never been particularly keen on accountancy. I studied taxation rather than accounting during my first degree and master's. But I was assigned to the accounting department as an intern when I first joined Huawei. Now, it's been more than 10 years and I'm still here. I am obsessed with detail. And this personality trait has turned out to be a plus for an accountant!

Making a Difference by Doing the Simple Things

My first job was dealing with employee expense claims. Back in 2000 we did not yet have the Self-Service Expense (SSE), an online system for claiming expenses. We had to process all claims and their supporting documents on paper. Every accountant's desk was piled high with forms and invoices. Each morning when you came to the office, you had to search through the mountains of paper to find the bits that you were supposed to deal with that day. If you found them the first time, it was cause for a celebration!

Eventually we just couldn't take it anymore. We put our heads together and invented a new way to handle all the paperwork: we divided up all the documents by category, and made a bin for each category of document, with notes to say who each piece of paper should flow to next. It was a brilliant system in theory, but we found that every time someone from outside our office came by, our meticulously ordered papers would end up in a complete mess.

Even more frustrating were muddled claims. Rather than making their expense claims straight away, some people would let them build up, then send in a whole bunch at once. They would arrive with invoices missing, invoices pasted to the wrong claim, different types of invoices all muddled together... completely unprepared for proper accounting. But we had to account for every penny of every claim with the correct invoices. Even a fifty cent bus ticket could not be wrongly recorded. We would get our calculators out and calculate back and forth to piece together exactly which invoices went together to make up exactly which expense claim. If you got a phone call in the middle of this process, there was a good chance you would have to start all over again. That would drive us crazy.

When we found problems with invoices, we would have to call the person who submitted the claim to tell them that they wouldn't receive the full amount. If they got angry, we then had to explain very carefully to try to make them understand. I used to get very worried about making those calls, but sometimes there was no way around it. I can still remember many occasions when I was trying to work out exactly how the expenses had come about with people who were already strained with the pressures of their work. Often, they would just refuse to go through all the different invoices and expenses because they had just forgotten everything, and would end up yelling at me. I felt that it was so unfair that I couldn't help crying sometimes. I even thought about quitting. Why should I have to take all this abuse?

I talked about it with my supervisor, and I still remember exactly what she said to me: "You're right. But have you thought about what you can do to change the situation? If you give up now, then you'll give up every time you find yourself faced with a tough challenge."

What she said pulled me out of my funk, and I stopped thinking about quitting. Instead, I focused on doing every task I was assigned to the best of my ability. When I became a manager myself, I often had to cheer up my team members when they were in the same situation that I had been in. You know the best way to overcome adversity? Hold on one more minute, and take one more step.

Later, the SSE system was launched. We taught everyone in the company how to choose the right category for their expenses and submit their claims in a timely manner. Later we made it a trust-based system, where we "pay first, check the paperwork later". Finally expense claims started to work right. Now staff can simply scan a QR code to upload their invoices, and the whole accounting process takes only an average of 2.6 days.

This was how we transformed our messy expense claim system from 10 years ago into the industry-leading SSE system today. However, it took a huge number of talented people to make it happen – just think of all the graduates and even the postgraduates we hired to work on the simple problem of dealing with employee expense claims. These talented people were able to look at the underlying problems and address them systematically and creatively. And this is what matters. That's why companies must invest in people, and give them responsibilities and opportunities. Talent is the ability to make a difference even when doing simple things.

Goodbye to Midnight Reconciliation

In 2001, I was assigned to the General Ledger Department, where monthly and annual financial reports were generated. Today, this department is an oasis of calm, where every accountant wants to work. But back then it was a whirlwind of chaos, always on the brink of disaster.

All of our overseas subsidiaries were using different financial software. Some used the ERP system, some used Peachtree, and others used Yonyou. Some outsourced the work to accounting firms. This meant we had to import all of the data manually into Excel spreadsheets every time we did accounting close. All financial reports, including the group's consolidated reports, were done in Excel. In Excel, the maximum worksheet size was about 68,000 rows, and that wasn't enough to accommodate all the data we put in. Dealing with so much data required that we master all of the spreadsheet functions, so we called ourselves the 'unbeatable Excel masters'.

There was another tricky problem: a code like '10010' might refer to one thing in Russia and another in Argentina. The data submitted from different sources came in many different forms, making consolidation impossible. So I had to create a reference so that we could convert all the different data into one single format for consolidation.

The consolidation of financial data is a rather complex concept. For example, imagine Huawei Technologies sells a product to Huawei Germany, and then Huawei Germany sells it to a customer. For the whole group, there's only one transaction, which means that to consolidate our books, the transaction between Huawei Technologies and Huawei Germany must be reconciled and eliminated.

The problem was that the books would not reconcile. Huawei Technologies said that it sold products worth CNY100 million to Huawei Germany. But Huawei Germany only had records of CNY1 million. In this case, I would have to go and ask Huawei Germany, "We shipped products worth CNY100 million, but why was only CNY1 million registered in your books?" To find out what had gone wrong, I had to go through the transaction step by step to find out exactly where the problem had arisen.

The probability of a successful monthly accounting close on the first attempt was like winning the lottery, close to zero. But we had to solve every problem before the reports were due on the 13th day of each month. Each month we would have nights when we were still in the office at 4am, working in shifts around the clock to check every piece of data. We were always in a state of high anxiety, and we started to dream about doing calculations for accounts and finding problems in the data.

Now that I am the president of the Accounting Management Department, I can say with confidence that this kind of situation almost never occurs today. We have been through years of improvement, and we now have a clear 'operational map' on which we detail each step during every hour of the accounting close process: what should be done at each step, what each department does, how people coordinate with each other, etc. When something goes wrong, it shows up immediately, like a flashing red light, and we can immediately take remedial action. We are going to make this 'operational map' more high-tech and more intuitive using a graphical interface.

How Accurate Are Your Financial Reports?

Although we worked very hard, we were still unable to produce financial reports on time, and when we did finally grind out the reports, their accuracy was often questioned.

Once, a budget manager asked me, with the latest reports in his hands, "We have signed the contract for that project in Russia. Why has it not shown up in the books?" I didn't have an answer to his question, so I tracked down the relevant finance manager and asked him why. He said, "I'm so sorry. That data is from two months ago. I haven't been to Russia over the last two months, so I didn't record the new project in the books."

On another occasion, many people came and told me the data in our reports was wrong because the revenue of one project was not correct. We did an analysis, and found that one single cable sale had been recorded in several different places. The project was actually a loss-maker, but as soon as the cable was shipped and accepted, the multiple revenue it generated had made the whole project look profitable. The problem here was that the business side had given us the wrong data, and we just entered it into the books because we had no idea there was a problem. But our books could easily give everyone a misleading impression.

Back then, I was in charge of the department. I felt terrible when I heard people complain about the quality of our reports. We just couldn't get good data, and although we were not causing the problems, we were the ones releasing the reports. When people found an error in the books, their first thought was that Finance hadn't done their job properly.

So what could we do to improve things? We realized that it was not enough to just manage our books. We had to look beyond our own business. We set up a dedicated team with more than a dozen people to find problems in our incoming data streams, and to go to other departments to sort them out. They had to be both our microscope, examining the financial data in minute detail, and our telescope, finding problems in the field, so that we could make the necessary adjustments.

However, this system didn't work very well. The problem was a steady flow of muddy data. Trying to filter it into a pure stream at the very last step was a fool's errand. It was like the water in the Yangtze River: when there is pollution upstream, you can never get clean water downstream. We realized that we must embrace the challenge, or we would be stuck in the same situation forever. So we stepped out into the business side to try to resolve the problems with data quality at the source, and make the whole process flow more smoothly.

When Huawei started using an external auditor, the urgency of the problem became even clearer. "What was this large sum for? Where is the contract? How long will this project take?" Back then, we used to just look at the figures and make our calculations. We didn't have any idea what was behind all those figures. We couldn't answer any of the questions raised by the auditor, so we spent hours calling up people on the business side to ask about the background.

The auditor had to make a lot of adjustments to early drafts of our financial reports. We couldn't even understand some of the adjustments. The auditor helped us write the footnotes to the financial reports, because we didn't know how we should state those reports. I still remember in 2001, when we had completed the audit of the group financial reports, I spent two weeks figuring out all the adjustments and the stories behind the numbers. I spent a whole day finishing a 40-page-long report explaining all the adjustments, and at the end of it I found that I was so tired I couldn't lift my arms. But I felt relieved, because I knew that next year we would have at least one person who could understand the auditor's adjustments.

IBM Teaches Us Shared Services

We were determined to make a change. Starting in 2005, the accounting department planned a series of transformation projects. There was a 'Four Ones' project (one organization, one IT system, one process, one group of human resources) that aimed to bring consistency to our global accounting policies, processes, and chart of accounts. Our ERP project developed a single accounting system for all overseas Huawei companies, and we established seven accounting shared service centres (SSCs) outside of China.

These projects were not easy undertakings. You had to be there to know just how difficult they were. Take the ERP upgrade in Brazil for example: it took four attempts before the system was finally working properly. In 2005, when we first rolled out the Huawei ERP system, we ran a detailed analysis of the Brazilian accounting and tax compliance rules and concluded that the system simply wouldn't support the local rules. We needed to develop a new system specifically for the Brazil Office. But we also had to make the system compatible with the company's IT architecture, and internal rules meant that the project was shelved for a long time. In 2006, the accounting department took the lead and deployed software called MICROSIGA. But again, this system didn't meet our needs, because the categories and level of detail didn't match our business processes. Two more projects followed. Finally, in April 2011, through the joint efforts of the business side, IT, finance, and the accounting departments, an ERP system was successfully launched in Brazil. All the project team members and other people who had worked on this project over the past six years were overcome with joy when the system finally came online.

While deploying ERP systems, we were also building up our ex-China accounting team. I remember in 2005, an IBM consultant gathered us in a large lecture hall, and explained to us what shared services were all about. He said that shared services meant spinning off the finance and human resource activities in all the different business units and setting up an independent entity to provide these services. Many renowned multinationals such as Ford, HP, and IBM had established accounting SSCs that provided high-quality, cost-effective, and consistent financial services to all the companies in these groups.

Upon hearing this, we looked at each other, totally at a loss. We couldn't even ask any questions. SSCs seemed to be way beyond anything we could understand. How could we do accounting for our subsidiaries if we didn't go to the countries to find out about the local rules? What if an invoice went missing, if the applicant didn't send it through to the finance department? Without the 24/7 access to finance on-site, how would the business side cope?

Luckily, the IBM consultants were very patient. They led us into the world of shared services. We started our journey with the seven accounting SSCs, although we were far from sure that they would succeed. I later managed the accounting SSCs in China and Argentina. And I came to understand what shared services were about: accounting SSCs are like a well-constructed dam. They control the flow of highly repetitive paperwork, delivering higher efficiency, compliance controls, and cost controls. They also save money and provide better services. SSCs are managed directly by HQ, so they remain independent of the local company and provide more accurate data.

After years of hard work, Huawei has now shrugged off its old-fashioned approach to global business, and has turned itself into a digital company. Now we can place an order in Victoria Island with a single click, and it will be quickly received by the Shenzhen Supply Center back in China, where it is processed immediately. The seven accounting SSCs take advantage of the different time zones to keep our accounts running close to 24/7.

That means our offices around the world can get the data they need at the fastest possible speed.

Breaking Down the Barriers between Accounting and Business

Once the ERP systems and accounting SSCs were up and running, we had a single IT system, and a globally integrated organization. However, we were still very detached from the business side. We still didn't know the stories behind the numbers, and the business side wasn't interested in the issues that troubled us. We still had many problems to deal with.

For example, say we signed a contract worth CNY100 million with a customer. The system recorded that we had shipped goods worth CNY100 million. The finance department would then issue an invoice for CNY100 million, and record a receivable of the same amount for collection. However, the customer then changed the contract and only received goods worth CNY30 million. The business side didn't update the contract information on their end, and as a result, the system still showed a receivable of CNY100 million. As the finance team, we needed to accurately record the company's profits, so we had to frequently ask the business side questions: Have you changed the contract? Have you disposed of the inventory after project closure? Have you collected the pre-payment from the contractors? It was a major pain.

One time, Ren Zhengfei was visiting a customer in Saudi Arabia and the customer asked him in confusion, "Why doesn't Huawei collect payment from us after finishing our project?" Mr Ren Zhengfei repeated these words to us in finance. He didn't criticize us or say anything else. But these words alone were enough to make the whole receivables team cry. The reason was that goods were shipped from China to Huawei Saudi Arabia, and Huawei Saudi Arabia then delivered the goods to the customer. We were supposed to nail down the unit prices with the customer, then look at the total quantity of equipment installed at each base station, and so issue a final invoice. However, we had completed the project, but we didn't have a list of the quantities of equipment and materials approved by the customer. So now it was time to invoice, but we even didn't know the quantities, which were required to determine the amount of the invoice.

The Integrated Financial Services (IFS) transformation that we launched in 2007 helped us out of the quagmire. IBM consultants helped Huawei establish a workbench for finance, which put in place smooth-flowing pipelines for finance data. The new system enabled everyone on the business side to know which of their activities must be recorded, and which information would flow to finance for inclusion in our financial reports. Now all of our business activities and data were flowing through pre-defined pipes. It turned out that it was not enough for the business side to know the rules. They didn't have detailed instructions on how to carry out each process, so there were still major problems with the quality of data. We had built the pipelines, but the water flowing through them was dirty. This was why we then launched another project in 2013, to improve internal controls on financial reporting. We started with our financial reports, and identified the key business activities on which we needed good data for the reports. We then set up metrics for getting good, clean data, and worked with the business side to monitor the metrics and make improvements as necessary. Gradually, we extended this approach to the front-end processes, so that the language spoken by the business side finally matched up with what we used in accounting.

From this point onwards, we had a channel of communication through to the business side. They started to understand that financial reports were not just a product of the finance department. Financial reports were made by everyone in the company. Things that they did that they weren't even aware of all fed into the financial reports. Once everyone understood this, they started working with us to proactively fix problems, and help us reflect our needs in their work. This allowed us to jointly produce the most accurate possible financial reports.

"Producing Financial Reports One Day Earlier Could Earn US$100 Million"

One of our senior executives once told us, "Producing financial reports one day earlier could earn us 100 million dollars. Reports allow us to look into the future, instead of looking back at the past." Faster reporting can help the company to make quicker decisions and seize future opportunities.

In Huawei's early days, we had no financial reports and we didn't know how much money we were making or losing. Then we started doing monthly financial reporting. The business was half done, but we still didn't know how we had performed last month. Today, we are able to release a full set of reports within five days, and we can view our operating reports on our laptops or phones any time. We should be proud of ourselves: the accounting and financial reporting services provided by Huawei's accounting SSCs now represent the best in the industry.

We have more achievements to be proud of: the cost of processing an invoice has been reduced by 75%, and adjustments made by our auditor are now as low as 0.01% of our data. Since 2014, we have run compliance checks on data flowing from the business side and caught issues in data amounting to US$7.8 billion. By catching these issues early, we have prevented up to US$945 million in losses.

Most importantly, each of our transformation programs has helped us to develop our people. Key team members involved in the transformations are now aware of the importance of end-to-end integration. They have learned to examine our problems and diagnose which processes are not working smoothly. This experience is the most precious thing we have gained from the transformations.

Still a Long Way to Go

Looking back, the accounting department has grown with the company. There have been many hardships and difficulties, but we have achieved breakthrough after breakthrough, and gained valuable experience along the way. The development of the accounting department has been the result of the hard work and innovation of everyone there. It is also a mirror of how Huawei has embraced challenges and forged ahead.

Looking into the future, the company will continue to grow. We will develop new businesses, new business domains, and new business models. Against this backdrop, how can our books accurately reflect the realities of our business and support our success? How can we continue to create robust financial reports as our business grows? How can we stay true to our basic principles, improve on our own ability to stay compliant, and provide oversight as we serve the business? How can we produce the most accurate possible books, help to increase profits, and become the best accounting practitioners in the ICT industry? To find the answers to all of these questions, we will need to work together. We can always progress by embracing the challenges before us.

The Weight of Responsibility

By Zheng Aizhu,
Chen Yan,
Wen Zeju,
Xu Shuang
and Tao Naihui

At Huawei, there is a team of accountants who are dedicated to the accuracy and veracity of financial data, and view these goals as important as life itself. They are down-to-earth and practical people. They selflessly support the interests of the company and are not afraid of getting on someone's bad side in the process, if it means sticking to principles. They have an incredible ability to hone their craft. After all, there isn't any payment too small not to care about. Not a single penny can be misplaced. They have laser-like precision in their work, and nothing gets past their vigilant gaze as they seek to keep the books in order. They are found in all parts of the world, working to clear overdue payments and recover losses for the company...

There aren't any exceptionally captivating stories to be told. But behind their effort is a calm, tempered, and ceaseless devotion to their objectives. A decade can pass in what seems like an instant. This group of people exhibits their sense of responsibility by never compromising, by always being proactive, and by seeking clarity in every respect possible.

Whether it was back in the day, when each person worked with their own calculator and manually processed paperwork, or today, where the entire process is streamlined end-to-end (what we like to call "the era where humans dance with machines"), accountability and responsibility have always been the prized objectives.

The weight of responsibility provides both the power and momentum for us to progress forward, slowly but surely. While it isn't anything flashy, it still has its own innate glow. It may not be all that eye-catching, but it is long-lasting, and it is important.

Establishing Order in a Tumultuous World
By Zheng Aizhu

I might be considered Huawei's first cashier.

When the company was founded, Mr Ren Zhengfei invited my husband Zhang Zhongshi and me on multiple occasions to join Huawei. We were very conflicted about the decision. In the city of Liyang, Guizhou Province, my husband was a middle manager at a state-owned enterprise and enjoyed some pretty nice perks with his job. He had a family to feed. It wasn't an easy choice to give up such a comfortable and steady government position.

Mr Ren Zhengfei implored us repeatedly to think about the future prospects of China's reforms and opening up. Eventually, we decided to take our fate into our own hands and choose the best path forward. The most attractive choice was to follow our dreams. It was at that time that we made the most important decision of our lives, and took an unforgettable new step.

On 4 February, 1989, we decided to give up our cosy government jobs. So we found ourselves, with our son, on a train heading to Guangzhou. We spent a night on an empty train, and by 6 February at noon (which was the beginning of the Chinese New Year), we reached Shenzhen, the home of Huawei. We gave every penny of our savings to Mr Ren Zhengfei, a grand total of 8,000 Chinese yuan. Mr Ren Zhengfei put in 7,000 yuan of his own, bringing the amount to 15,000 yuan. This was the original start-up capital for Huawei. From that point onward, our fates were forever tied to Huawei.

The company only had three departments at the time: the Research & Production Department, the Marketing Department, and the Office. My major in university was related to precision instrumentation, which didn't help much in the role I was taking at the company. But Mr Ren Zhengfei trusted me completely, and put me in charge of the finances. I was all too aware of the weight of the responsibility given to me. But I never flinched.

Back then, the company didn't have any finance policies. I just followed one simple rule: no matter how high your station in the company, you had to deal honestly with the finances. Some of the people working in the Marketing Department were somewhat careless in how they handled invoices. But I stood like a brick wall, demanding that everything be kept clear and accurate. I remember one time in particular when a company leader returned from a business trip. He pulled all his invoices from taxis and hotels out in a huge handful from his pocket and asked me to help him sort it all out. He wasn't being intentionally unhelpful, and did give all his invoices to me. I carefully verified each invoice, and during this process I discovered some personal expenses had been included. For example, he had provided an invoice for his children's tuition fees, for book fees, and other such expenses. I took all of these out, and told him that such expenses couldn't be reimbursed. He laughed, then answered, "I like how you work. If you're not even willing to reimburse those expenses for us higher-ups, then I'm sure other people aren't reimbursing things they shouldn't be!"

Before computers became common in the workplace, we did the books by hand. I would help the accountants to carefully get all the accounts in order. We had to know exactly how much money we had taken in, and how much money we had spent. We couldn't be off by a single penny, and we had to issue our financial reports quickly and accurately. Especially for our expenditure, signatures and stamps had to be obtained from me before any payments were made.

In 1991, our offices got computers. The company arranged for me and Zhen Xiaohua to develop a financial system ourselves. The system had to include incoming materials, received payments, expenditure, and other details, aiming to increase efficiency. I was entirely computer illiterate, but had to get up to speed with the technology in order to get the job done, and done right.

With our financial system in place, we saw a significant increase in efficiency. But the accuracy and timeliness of the data still relied heavily on the sense of responsibility of each individual. I checked the computer data that year line-by-line myself.

Looking back on it all now, if I were asked to name a positive tradition at Huawei, our financial handling would be one of them. Since the founding of the company, Huawei has always been dedicated to maintaining the veracity of our accounts. We used to rely solely on a sense of responsibility. But today, in addition to responsibility, we also have well-designed processes and mechanisms in place to ensure our accounts are up to snuff.

Although I have since retired, when I see how well Huawei has done in the marketplace, I still feel an enormous sense of pride.

Zheng Aizhu joined Huawei in 1989, and previously held posts including corporate cashier and Huawei Hong Kong cashier. Zheng retired in 2004.

Every Penny Counts
By Chen Yan

In 1998, the Chinese mainland was still very much under-developed. Each month when paying out employee salaries, a cashier had to go to a bank and collect the cash. Each bill had to be counted and delivered into the hands of every employee.

To make sure each of our thousands of employees received their salary on the 15th of every month, an essential skill of a cashier was quickly and accurately counting and recording cash amounts. As a newcomer, my learning started with counting bills one-by-one and doing mental calculations. I worked on my math skills every chance I got, even when having a meal. I caught myself doing math in my sleep. I eventually got a firm handle on the job. Newly minted bills were crisp and straight, and could be counted more easily with a lick of a finger. If new bills and older bills were mixed together, they could get caught together in the bill counter, so it made sense to straighten them all out before beginning your counts. There were also all sorts of mental tricks you could use to make the work easier, and to keep the numbers straight in your head.

The 15th of every month was our busiest time. Production Line 1 was in Xixiang. We had to conduct an inventory, divide up the cash, and travel to Xixiang to deliver the cash into the hands of employees. Other staff had to visit the finance office to collect their salaries. That entire day, all that could be heard in the finance office was the sound of bills being counted, and the 'clack-clack-clack' of calculators. Our hands never rested because we were so busy counting bank notes, sending them to employees' hands, verifying this-or-that, conducting inventories, and keeping a handle on unclaimed cash. We had to make sure the books lined up with the reality of our business. We also had to regularly respond by telephone to employee inquiries about their salaries.

Owing to the long lines and the expectant and happy eyes of the employees, we were always looking for ways to speed things up. We only allowed ourselves time to breathe once we had delivered the exact amount of salary down to the penny into each employee's hands. Only when we had finished our work would we often find that our voices were hoarse, our hands sore, and fingers parched. Some days we didn't even take the time for a sip of water.

Those days were tough. We were always thinking about how to continue to improve efficiency. One thing we thought of was to use voice calls like the way telephone banking works, allowing staff to inquire about their salaries using an automated system. With support from the company's IT staff, in about three months' time Huawei developed its own automated telephone system for employee salary inquiries. After entering their work ID and a password, employees could obtain automated information about their salary.

But this was only the beginning. During a discussion one day with a bank, I happened to hear them mention a new service they were offering. Companies were now able to have the bank remit salaries directly to employee bank accounts. The bank could pay employee salaries on the company's behalf? This was more convenient for employees, as it would save them from having to line up every month to collect cash.

When I heard about the idea, I felt like I'd died and gone to heaven. After considerable discussion and comparisons of various options, we ultimately decided upon Bank of China as our pilot service provider for salary issuances. In July 1999, the bank sent staff to help production employees open the first series of salary bank accounts.

Even though it was now the bank that was issuing the salaries, every detail of every line of numbers still had to be carefully checked. We couldn't let our guard down for a moment, since behind every row of data was the hard-earned salary of every employee. After receiving the salary data for the current month, we would immediately begin to sort through, check and confirm it, and submit the reports for approval. Then we would issue checks, encrypt the data, and send it off to the bank. On the 15th of the month, the first batch of salaries issued through the bank were sent to employee accounts. There wasn't a single error, and some employees even called to express their gratitude for the service.

So now employee salaries were being issued through the bank. Was there also a better way to handle supplier and employee reimbursements and payments? I brought these thoughts with me on a business trip to the frontline overseas. At that time, daily payments were done by a cashier filling out a stack of checks and transfer slips by hand. Then they had to find someone with approval authority to sign-off on the paperwork. Next, they had to bring the transfer slips to the bank, wait in line, and handle the transfer manually at the bank counter. Upon receiving the checks, the supplier or employee would also have to go to a bank counter to get the money. This was a very inefficient way of doing things, took a long time, and just felt wrong.

After giving the issue a lot of thought, our team came up with the idea of using online banking to make the payments. It was a very satisfying day for me when I finally saw those stacks of checks turned into electronic payment orders, and securely and quickly transferred to an online banking system.

In 2008 the online banking system was launched globally. In 2010, the host-to-host payment system, giving direct connectivity between Huawei and the Industrial and Commercial Bank of China, was deployed, and in 2011 the host-to-host system using SWIFT codes came online. Today, over 90% of payments are done electronically. The company's payment system has gradually developed into an intelligent system that is far removed from its beginnings as a manual ledger and self-developed system of accounting. The differences in settlement details between banks around the world are now also recorded in a standardized system, rather than us having to rely on individual memories and passing on of information orally.

In the eyes of many, handling payments is tedious and monotonous work. But there is no payment too small not to worry about. Payments are linked to procurement, delivery, HR, funding, and many other processes. They are also a direct link to suppliers, employees, banks, customers, and other internal and external stakeholders in the industry. Only by constantly honing our skills and maintaining our sense of responsibility can we better support the business.

Chen Yan joined Huawei in 1998, and has previously held positions at the company in the Corporate Funds Department, Cashier Department, and the United Arab Emirates Accounting Shared Services Center. Chen Yan is currently overseeing global payments.

The SSE Assistant Closest to You
By Wen Zeju

In early 2008, I was put in charge of the Self Service Expense (SSE) hotline for employee expense claims. We were responsible for responding to inquiries about expense claims from 80,000 employees in China. Prior to this, these inquiries were handled by various accountants. For the same question, employees might receive different answers from different accountants, and would have trouble obtaining an authoritative answer. It was also tough to find the right person to answer some questions. Making matters worse was the fact that accountants also had their day jobs to tend to. Reviewing expense claims and trying to answer questions at the same time just wasn't the most efficient and effective way of doing things.

I got straight down to work with another colleague. When we first started, all we knew was that accountants were receiving countless inquiries all day and every day. But no one had bothered to assess these inquiries to see how many there actually were and what was being asked. Sometimes ignorance is bliss. We applied for a shared e-mail box to collect all inquiries into a single space, and changed our landline numbers to the hotline inquiry number. Then we distributed this centralized information to all employees in the Chinese mainland.

That same day, my office landline became the expense claim hotline for every single employee in China.

"My business travel accommodation receipt was ruined in the washing machine. The amount is no longer visible. How can I get reimbursed?"

"The office moved to a new location. According to local conventions, we had a local monk come to pray and bless the office. Can I reimburse that?"

"The office administration bought two dogs to protect the residence building. How should I reimburse that expense?"

...

I can't tell you how many strange questions I have fielded. If you can think it, I've been asked it. After a few months, I had greeted people over the phone with "Hello, how may I help you" tens of thousands of times. I also became a walking dictionary for information about the company's expense policies.

Back then there was no case study database to rely on, nor any knowledge base. The finance hotline was a hodgepodge of common sense, personal experience, and a little luck. A colleague and I would split the day up in the morning and afternoon, one of us fielding telephone calls and the other handling e-mails. Upon receiving a call from an employee, we would record the employee's work ID and a summary of their question into an Excel spreadsheet. For simple questions, we would provide an answer over the phone. For tougher issues, we would respond later by e-mail or telephone. It was often the case that another call would ring in immediately after we put the receiver down. We didn't even have a chance to catch our breath. At the end of the day, it was common for us to find ourselves dry-mouthed and exhausted. We would often neglect to grab a drink of water or hit the washroom all afternoon.

Two accountants weren't enough to support the development of the company moving forward. We had to build an SSE service platform as quickly as possible, moving commonly fielded employee inquiries onto the SSE homepage. This would enable us to guide employees in finding information themselves, and help them quickly resolve issues.

We would work during the day receiving calls and answering e-mails. Then, in the evenings, we would work overtime and summarize the types of questions we had received, put together a compendium of standardized information, and send them to all employees. We designed the self-service platform with employee experience in mind, putting together guides and case studies based on different roles within the company, including for new employees and managers.

In less than six months, we had set up a self-service platform on the SSE homepage, which is still used right up to this day. In 2014, upon the foundations of the SSE hotline, we linked up the financial payment hotline on a global scale. As the system has been continuously improved, today more than 95% of financial payment inquiries can be resolved by employees themselves using the automated service. In 2016, the SSE application was launched, enabling employees to make inquiries about financial payment issues on their mobile phones whenever and wherever they desire.

In June 2016, following a major change in tax handling requirements prescribed by the Chinese government – a transition from business taxes to value-added taxes – we worked with staff involved in tax and IT to quickly provide a mobile inquiry function for invoice issuance information. I happened to be away on business at the time, and was very confident that I would be able to show the hotel staff the information I needed them to add to the accommodation invoice in order for me to get reimbursed. Unfortunately, however, my Wi-Fi connection was acting up, and after 15 minutes of trying, I couldn't get the process completed online. I regretfully realized that sometimes a plan that seems perfect in one's own eyes can still present many shortcomings in reality. On my way back to Shenzhen, I was constantly thinking about how to remedy the issue. A month later, the new functionality was officially launched, enabling rapid and accurate invoice issuing. The application supported QR code scanning and delivery of invoice information by e-mail to merchants; it also supported offline inquiries. This finally addressed many of the issues relating to invoice issuance that had long plagued employees.

Over the years, we have worked to streamline SSE systems, simplify processes, and build a robust and useful platform. We place trust in employees, providing payment of expenses before final review of invoices. We support mobile rapid reimbursement of expenses whenever and wherever the employee chooses to submit a request. We also allow employees to sign off on paperwork themselves prior to final filing. By working with procurement staff, we have optimized the self-purchase process for low-value goods and services, and have centralized all expense claim requests onto the SSE. Even electronic invoices can now support expense claims. Of course, the ideal situation would be if there was no need for expense claims at all. We are now working with business departments to extend company payment of expenses across a larger scope within the company.

The accounts payable (AP) hotline still has a long way to go in terms of agent support and smart location of case studies. This is a result of technological restrictions as well as limited resources. But I am confident that in the near future, employee expense claims or inquiries about payment problems will be as easy as saying "one, two, three". The automated service will be available 24/7 and will meet the real needs of staff in a thoughtful and friendly manner.

It is my true and firm belief that the biggest responsibility I have is to get my job done right, one step at a time. I have to do the best job I can, and focus on employee needs while ensuring business runs smoothly.

Wen Zeju joined Huawei in 2006, and has worked at the Mauritius Accounting Shared Services Center, and the Accounting Business Controls Department. Wen is currently in charge of overseeing employee expenses globally.

Leaving No Stone Unturned in Pursuit of an Accurate Accounting Record
By Xu Shuang

In 2013, company leadership decided to acquire a company in country X. At the time, I was the country's chief accountant. I therefore joined the project team to oversee finance work relating to the acquisition. The project schedule was really tight. We had one week to complete on-site checks, and two weeks to complete a due diligence investigation and a detailed post-merger integration plan. Then we had a month to complete contract preparation and negotiations...

The biggest challenge wasn't just time. Back then, the investment process within the company wasn't well developed. There were basically no documents to guide financial handling. We had no guidance on what the due diligence investigations should focus on, how to assess an acquisition agreement, or how to design a post-merger integration plan. Everything had to be done ad hoc.

While I had never participated directly in a merger before, I did have experience undergoing one. Two years prior, our subsidiary in country X had acquired a company, and there had been countless problems, extending from internal processes to external compliance. The CFO and I spent unbelievable amounts of energy and time picking up the pieces of that mess. If the present project wasn't handled right, we might be sitting on a ticking time bomb. All in an instant, it seemed that countless questions and concerns began popping up. I became anxious, and was losing sleep.

The most important thing to do before a merger is the due diligence investigation. The idea behind the investigation is to learn as much as possible about the target company, to provide a basis for future decision-making. However, amidst an ocean of information, what should we focus on? The next day, I began to study the target company's financial statements. As I read through them, I discovered that the company's circumstances were similar to those of the company I had dealt with two years prior. They were involved in similar businesses, and faced very similar issues. The lessons I had learned from the past gave me the knowledge I needed to make a breakthrough in the project! I went through the statements and information about the company once again, and quickly focused my attention on a few key points.

In order to get a fuller picture of the company, I listed out all the relevant companies that had gone through mergers in recent years in various countries, and inquired into each of them with local chief accountants, asking the same question: "What problems did you guys run into?" With this information in hand, plus my own professional judgment, I was able to put together a targeted due diligence checklist.

Four days later, I was at the target company holding very useful discussions with the company's CEO and finance staff. We got all the finance-related information we needed within half a day. The information on hand was enough to complete a due diligence report.

However, at the same time, some key risks had emerged. The biggest problem was that the company had never undergone an independent audit. Internal financial process controls were relatively simple, and there were dangers associated with the accuracy, completeness, and fairness of the numbers. This was directly linked to what price should be set for the acquisition. In addition, the post-merger integration of the company's business was a job even more complex than the investigative report itself. We would have to have detailed information to support plan design and implementation. Therefore, the due diligence investigation had to go deeper.

The next thing I did was hang around the target company's office for two days reading through a mountain of contracts and documents. I learned everything I could about the company's management, employees, the company providing accounting services to them, and the target company's banks. I finally gained confidence in my understanding of the company's receipts, expenditures, assets, and liabilities as reported in their financial statements. I also obtained detailed information about the company's bank account management, supplier payments, salary payments, tax return filings, and other financial activities. I analysed and discussed the information I gathered with experts in various fields.

Based on the information I obtained from my investigation, I uncovered key issues during the subsequent process of assessing the acquisition agreement. There was a difference in understanding between the parties regarding acquisition price during the negotiations, which led to a major variance in the amounts being sought. In addition, the debt repayment between the company and its original shareholders wasn't clearly arranged. Some question marks in all of this would directly influence our company's cash expenditures in the acquisition, as well as our tax costs. After raising these issues, the project team pulled together experts in law, tax, and consulting to discuss and eliminate the risks.

Thanks to our comprehensive investigation, our financial integration plan was very detailed and well adapted to this deal. Within two weeks of the formal acquisition, the target company completed key processes relating to funds, salaries, procurement, and accounts. Everything went off without a hitch, and no major hiccups occurred in business operations. Internal and external compliance risks were all kept under control.

Looking back on the project, I see now that it was because of our prudent attitude toward financial data and processes that we were able to achieve such a thorough understanding of the data and details. With this attitude, we were able to realize our mission: to effectively support business operations and control financial risks.

Xu Shuang joined Huawei in 2007, and has worked in the Reporting Center and Romania Accounting Shared Services Center. Xu Shuang is now the manager of a team overseeing group reporting and analysis.

Recovering Revenue for the Company
By Tao Naihui

In late December 2015, as I was wrapping up my reconciliation work for an office and about to finish an epic 270-day business trip, I received a telephone call that entirely threw me off the rails.

"Hold on a little while longer!" To minimize its long overdue receivables, the office wanted to work with the telecom operator in the province and re-check its accounts again. Upon hearing this, my heart dropped faster and further than the snow falling outside my window. I was only an airplane ticket away from home, but all of a sudden I became sorely aware of the immensity of the ocean separating me from my family.

Nonetheless, I was more sure than anyone else that if the books were not clear, then there were certain to be future issues with collecting payments from customers. There would be inaccuracies in the accounts. We would also run into other commonly seen major issues, including long overdue receivables and abnormal prepayments from customers. If we could nip the problems in the bud and get the numbers cleared up in the first place, then those future problems could be avoided, and the company could be saved from incurring further losses. As I thought about this, I became resolved to face the tasks and challenges at hand.

For historical reasons, the business data between the telecom operator in the province and Huawei became impossible to match up, beginning in 2010. Old problems were buried by new ones, which grew into further problems. It was a true Gordian Knot, which we were tasked with unravelling. To make matters worse, contracts were dispersed all over the province in various cities.

If we wanted to reconcile the books, we would have to travel throughout that province.

I was aware of the challenges ahead. We were looking up at a very tall and very steep peak. But it was going to be climbed, one step at a time. Working with two other colleagues at the Shared Services Center, I got down to business right away with reconciliation work for each city in the province. Each morning at about 7am we boarded a plane destined for a different city, and around 11pm returned to our accommodations. When we got back to our rooms, we organized that day's results and began preparing the materials needed for the next day.

I ran into a major problem when reconciling the numbers in one city. Because the customer didn't have a dedicated person overseeing finance, we weren't able to directly conduct reconciliation. We could only reconcile with an engineer responsible for reporting of accounts. It was coming up to the end of the year, and the customer simply didn't have the time to worry about what we were doing. There wasn't anything we could do but wait around and seize spare moments in the customer's schedule to get things done. Early each morning, we would head to the customer's offices. When they were otherwise occupied, I would busy myself by organizing data. When I noticed they had some time on their hands, I would brazenly interrupt them to verify a contract or two.

After doing this for almost three days, I realized something important. The engineer wasn't looking at system records at all. The data given to me were payment records being maintained in individual notebooks. There was no way to guarantee the accuracy of the numbers. This made me very nervous. I raised this issue multiple times, but received a single answer: "Aren't you just trying to reconcile the numbers? Isn't it enough that I give you those numbers?"

Yes, it was true that I was just trying to match up the numbers, but behind those numbers were each of the company's receivables. Each line represented value that could be recovered by the company. I had to ensure that each of the reconciled numbers could equate to a successful payment to the company. Numbers that couldn't be matched up required follow-up to find out the cause, and to push for resolution. The ultimate aim was to standardize business operations and execution. Time restraints simply wouldn't allow us to continue along this inefficient path. If the numbers themselves were problematic, how could we rely on the results?

As I thought about this, I decided to take an unusual path, and to take a quick and effective approach to re-check the numbers. Luckily for me, we were able to obtain a portion of the data from the telecom operator's provincial branch. By having the engineer verify the numbers on-site, and with validation on the system data, I was able to complete all contract verifications and ascertain where the variances lay. Through constant communication, the provincial branch finally agreed to routinely provide province-wide data. Moving forward, not only would it be easier to confirm the accuracy of the customer's data, but there would also be less need to make so many trips to each city, thus making our work much more efficient.

In 2016, the office received nearly 10 million yuan in repayments from the customer. I was really happy about that. I had lived up to my responsibilities over the prior 300 days. To me, responsibility means getting routine jobs done, and done well. Going the extra mile makes a huge difference.

Tao Naihui joined Huawei in July 2012, and previously worked at the General Ledger Department of the Chengdu Accounting Shared Services Center. In March 2015, Tao Naihui started to work on sales accounting at the Chengdu Accounting Shared Services Center.

An
Apprenticeship
on the Roof of
the World

By Zhang Xinrui

In the summer of the year I turned 22, I made a phone call to my mother. "Mom," I said, "I'm going to work in Nepal."

My mother didn't ask why or how. She just gave a little laugh and replied, "You just keep going further and further, don't you?"

It was true. I had left my small hometown for Peking University, then moved to Shenzhen, spent some time in Thailand, and now I was taking a permanent placement in Nepal. Every move took me further beyond my parents' control. Though my mother didn't know it, I'd had my sights set on working overseas ever since my first interview with Huawei. But not even I had imagined that I would end up spending so long in this little kingdom just over the Himalayas from China.

Plenty of Courage When You're Young

In June 2016, I had only been at Huawei for one year. One day I received a call from the CFO of the Huawei Nepal Office. "Would you be interested in coming out to Nepal to be a project financial

Zhang Xinrui on her graduation day

controller (PFC)? We are building a network for a local telecom operator. The project is very complex, and is losing money. It will be a big challenge, but that's the best way to learn."

Before I made my decision, I asked a colleague in Nepal what it was like working there. He gave me a very honest answer: "It's a bit primitive, and we have to work very hard indeed. But you learn a lot."

I was young and green. What I needed was experience. What I had in spades was courage. It was a simple decision: I was going!

The mountains around Kathmandu

On 6 July, 2016, I boarded a plane in Hong Kong, bound for Nepal. While I was still at the airport, I received a message from my new boss, the head of the accounts department responsible for the local operator. "Welcome to Nepal," he said. "I hope you're prepared. The projects we are doing are more complex than you could possibly imagine. Let's talk when you arrive and get you up and running as quickly as possible."

Another message came from the head of the Nepal Office: "Get familiar with the business as soon as possible. These projects are complex and many things are not settled. Past problems mean that there's a lot that needs doing. We need to keep the projects alive, and set them on a path to profitability – long-term, stable profitability."

I was a second year newbie. Could I really help turn around a loss-making project and make it profitable? This question didn't matter anymore. I had accepted the baton, and the next leg was mine to run.

No Stone Unturned: Unearthing the Ancient History of a Project

As it turned out, I was given no time at all to get up to speed with the operations of the project. The very first week I was there, I received an order: to determine the cause of a gap running into the millions between our invoices and accounts received, which had been left unexplained for more than a year. I had to resolve this gap in the accounts as quickly as possible. It all happened so fast my head was spinning.

Millions of dollars was no small sum. How could such a large gap have appeared between our invoices and our actual revenue? Were the payments late, or had the invoices not been issued on time? Were some invoices being issued too late? Could there have been errors made when preparing the invoices themselves? Countless questions spun around in my head.

There were 80 contracts covering the work we did during that time that I had to review. With the help of Huawei's Accounting Shared Services Center in Malaysia, I drew up a table that included all of the project milestones and the original schedule for invoicing, to help locate the differences between invoice amounts and recorded revenue. During this process, I started to realize how finance, as a backend function, provides oversight over the business side while ensuring that revenue is going into their pockets. When a gap opens up between the numbers, that means there is a potential risk. When the gap grows too large, that means we need to operate much more cautiously to control the risk.

I learned what was going on and gradually refined my table. When I didn't understand something, I'd send email after email until someone could explain it. If anyone failed to reply to me, I'd go knocking on doors until I found someone who could help, and we would fill in the details together and work out where the problems lay. In the end I was able to resolve almost all of the problems, until I was left with just eight contracts, worth nearly half a million dollars. But no one in the Nepal Office could help me with these. Everyone I asked said, "I wasn't here when those were signed, so I don't know what was happening." That was fair enough – some of the contracts went back to 2003, when I was still in elementary school!

If I couldn't get answers from my co-workers, then I would have to go and find the evidence myself. People may come and go, but numbers don't lie. For each of these eight contracts, I had to go back step by step: When were they logged onto our system? How was each contract divided into batches? When was each purchase order closed out? When did the revenue show up in the accounts? I asked the Shared Services Center to show me the accounting solution, and got the logs from the administrators of each separate IT system that these contracts flowed through. Many of the records had been lost, but I was able to find enough clues to demonstrate that this half a million dollars had actually been received; the records had got mixed up when one or other of the computer systems had been updated. It was this data error that was showing up in our accounts. Along the way, I also discovered a neglected network maintenance contract with US$130,000 in receivables that we could collect from the customer; and an old services contract worth US$600,000 that we had delivered but for which we had never obtained an acceptance certificate from the customer.

After a month of work, I finally saw a clean set of accounts in front of me. It was a sweet victory, and it was the first piece of work I had completed in Nepal. Along the way, I had learned about the various activities involving accounts receivable and payment collection, and I had met a lot of people with whom

I would work closely over the coming year. They got to know me, as well, and became more confident about coming to ask me for help with their finance questions. I felt that I had established myself as part of the team, and I turned from old contracts to the ongoing ones. I monitored the project's revenue and payments received. Gradually the risks associated with the differences between recorded revenue and invoice amounts were well under control.

Just a Database on Legs

When one old colleague had heard that a raw young recruit like me was being sent out to Nepal as a PFC, she gave me a warning: "Before you know it, they'll have you on turnkey projects."

Before I went to Nepal, I had only worked on one small fixed network project for two months. I only handled a few simple tasks. Now I had to manage the finances for a whole group of projects, involving processes from selecting places for base station construction to building communications towers and installing equipment, and products for wireless networks, transport networks, and fixed networks. I was encountering most of these processes for the first time, so I felt like I was stumbling my way through the dark. What was even more difficult was that I was not just looking after one project. I had to take care of the finances of the whole accounts department. And we were struggling to tidy up errors made in the past and manage significant losses on our services contracts.

It was hard to know where to start with this mess, so I turned to the tasks at hand. The first thing on my to-do list was to take over as chair of the department's weekly operation review meeting. That sounded simple enough. I already had a template for the meeting presentation, so surely all I had to do was to fill in last week's details. So that's what I did for my first meeting. But after 20 minutes, I'd finished reading out all the updates from last week, and I had no idea how to fill the rest of the 90-minute meeting. Fortunately, everyone filled the embarrassing silence with a discussion of the figures, and we managed to make it through an hour, at least. I listened carefully to everything my colleagues said, and tried to note it all down, but I couldn't keep up with the pace of the conversation. At the end of the meeting I felt rather frustrated. Finance people are supposed to be 'walking databases', but was that all of my function? To spit out lists of data?

I started to look carefully back over the past data, and worked out exactly how each figure was generated. But the deeper I got into the data, the more confused I felt. Exactly where were the losses coming from? What could I do to help the project teams operate more effectively? Feeling somewhat defeated, I went to seek help from the Nepal CFO. He gave me a piece of advice: "Go and talk to the people on the ground. Find out how the business really works, and then you'll find where you need to focus your energy."

I used every opportunity I had to find out about the projects and what had happened in the past. I sat with the head of the accounts department and listened to his plans, and used that to set my own priorities. Other colleagues were also very happy to share what they knew. One time I was having trouble understanding a project delivery plan, so I called up the VP for project delivery, and he spent several hours laying it out for me step by step. He filled a whole blackboard with diagrams, until finally I understood what the plan was about. But there's nothing like getting your hands dirty to help you understand what's going on. So whenever I had a moment, I went out with the project guys to the base stations and mucked in with the installation. I got to see first-hand how we delivered our products to the customer. Gradually, I began to see beyond the simple lists of numbers, and understood the targets that we were trying to achieve out there in the field.

Of course, understanding the numbers and the projects was just the first step. A PFC has to develop solutions for problems as well. September was always our busiest month, so at the start of the month, with the head of the accounts department and the project director at my back, I gathered together the core team to sort out our priorities. We started at 5pm, and didn't finish till half past three in the morning. For every KPI target, we worked out how we could hit that target over the last four months of the year, and ultimately produced a complete plan for the year end. Then we turned that plan into clear task descriptions. Where everything had been muddy, we created clarity. This was our contribution to more efficient management.

Over the next month, come rain or shine, the whole team came in an hour early every morning and updated our plan before work. I did my best to meet the Nepal Office's expectations of a PFC as well: I learned every step of the project delivery process, and found out what the company's business really consisted of. I took myself out of accounting's 'ivory tower', and started to take on responsibility for the projects under my purview. I was determined to not just be the numbers girl any more.

Budget Preparation: Baptism of Fire

In October, three months after I had arrived in Nepal, Huawei started its annual budget process. This meant that we would have to work out our operating budget, budget for strategic projects, cash flow budget, key risks, major budget assumptions, and a string of other tricky questions for the upcoming year. Everyone says that you're not a real PFC until you've been through the annual budget process, so I knew that I was about to have my eyes opened once again. I had handled budget sheets before, of course, but only for one project at a time. This was the first time I had had to draft a full budget for four separate projects that we were running for this particular customer. Inevitably, I was nervous, and struggled to get a grip on the job at first.

Our CFO gave us our orders: "I want first draft budget sheets in three days." Over the next two days, it seemed like the more I did, the more confused I became. I couldn't even get the revenue straight. On the third day I scrabbled together some kind of a complete version and delivered it to the CFO, who looked through it without any surprise. This was what he had expected, he said.

As we drafted our budgets, we thought to ourselves: projects are like rock climbing. If you haven't planned out your route to the summit properly, then you won't be able to correctly work out each step along the way.

Over the next three weeks, the CFO worked with us, going through the revenue, then the costs, then the tied-up capital. For me and the other PFCs, it was like being back at school. Each evening we would sit together, reviewing our progress, learning accounting rules, and helping each other get our respective project budgets up to date. We stayed till late at night, pausing for the odd midnight feast of instant noodles when needed. Through this real-world exercise, and with plenty of trial and error along the way, I finally learned how to prepare a budget.

Basic competence is one thing. Mastery of a skill is quite another: a different stage, and a different psychological state. As we drafted our budgets, we thought to ourselves: projects are like rock climbing. If you haven't planned out your route to the summit properly, then you won't be able to correctly work out each step along the way. That is even more true when your project is losing money. It's like dancing on a knife's edge. Every step requires extreme caution. Before that year, the Nepal Office had only ever developed one-year budgets for their projects. Now, over those three weeks of completing our budgets, the other PFCs and I went beyond that. We laid out a plan for the next three to five years, with recommendations for delivery strategies over

Finance team updating their budgets

the lifetime of our respective projects. We worked out what the optimal operating assumptions would be to enable us to satisfy our customers' needs.

We submitted our budgets for final review in fear and trepidation. But the response I got made me laugh with joy. "This year's budget is the clearest description of the operations of this customer that I have ever seen." All the tension of the past few weeks melted away the instant I heard that.

My first three months had been a period of experimentation and exploration. Now I had survived a baptism of fire through the budgeting process. Finally, I had found my centre. This process had taught me that finance requires more than just pushing numbers around. You have to make the accounts clear, and make them accurate. You have to be forward-looking and look at the work from end-to-end. You have to start with the customer's needs, then assign your resources, and develop the best budget assumptions to help improve operations, generate profits, and control risks.

Payment Collection Where Every Second Counts

In November a new problem arrived on my desk. Our department was supposed to collect on US$5 million in accounts payable that year after our project passed the customer's final acceptance inspections. Year end was coming up, and we had to work out how to make that happen.

It took a seemingly endless string of meetings and sign-offs by dozens of people at the customer company, but inch by inch we helped the department obtain its first final acceptance certificate (FAC) from this customer. I gained a new understanding of the phrase 'hard work' – and learned why FACs were spoken of with an almost superstitious awe. We were up against the clock, because the department had set year end as the deadline for getting the customer's payment and finally closing this long, hard project.

Our records suggested that even with the wind at our backs and no nasty surprises, the fastest we could do all this in was 45 days. Could we possibly hit our deadline?

Step 1: Simplify. Before we started, I called the finance team together, and we went over every step in the payment collection process, working out who needed to do what, what approvals they needed, and how long everything would take. We ran through everything over and over again, and came up with a baseline schedule for completing the payment collection process. We squeezed out all of the reducible delays, and wrote up a table which listed each payment we needed to collect, and how it was going to happen. Every evening, no matter how late it got, we would go over that table and check whether we were on schedule, or what had knocked us off before we went home for the night. Altogether, this process helped us shave 10 days off the process.

Step 2: Compress. We tried applying pressure to each of the so-called 'fixed' timings. Internally, I called up the treasury team at HQ and the manager in charge of payment collection in Nepal to discuss how we could shave time off our internal processes. For example, if you give payment request documents to the bank on Thursday, they would handle them the next business day; if you only give them to the bank on Friday, then you have to wait the whole weekend before they would be processed. That meant a gap of three days. So we pushed our people to get the FAC necessary for a payment request from the customer as early as possible to eliminate the gap. We also asked our account manager about the approval on the customer side. Over and over again we asked him, "Is there any chance that the process can be sped up? Would there be a delay?" As a result, we were able to get some of our processes to go in parallel. That knocked another four days off our baseline. But we could not see any way to cut out any more than those seven days. Now we had a new baseline timeline for payment collection of 28 days.

Could we make it even shorter? We decided to give it a try. On the afternoon of 24 November, our account manager finally collected our FAC from the customer's offices. I had a driver waiting outside the office, and he rushed the certificate back to the Huawei offices. Our invoicing team issued the invoice as soon as they laid eyes on the certificate, completed their internal checks overnight, and then hustled them off to HQ. When HQ arrived at work in the morning, they were able to send the invoice directly to the customer's bank to request payment. We kept a close eye on the mailing process and the progress of the bank's sign-off for the documents so that we were able to send them back to the customer as soon as possible. Thanks to the account manager's hard work, the customer's complex approvals were now running partly in parallel. Piece by piece, the process fell into place. Everyone stepped up smartly to play their role at exactly the right second, and in the end we collected our first payment upon final acceptance inspections just 18 days after we had started. That was nearly a full week ahead of our baseline schedule, and more than twice as fast as anyone had managed it before.

On 10 December, the head of our accounts department brought a payment order back from the offices and presented it to me. I couldn't help bursting into tears, and one of my colleagues managed to snap a rather unflattering photo of me! Everyone laughed at me for crying over such a small first payment.

Nepal finance team with some visiting colleagues

"Just wait till US$10 million comes in at the end of the month," they said, "that'll be worth crying over!" But for me it was the relief of seeing the payment process finally come to an end and the weight fall from my shoulders. I felt like I had reached the summit of a mountain.

On 31 December, we did indeed receive a payment of US$10 million, but I was very calm. "Aren't you going to cry?" they asked me, but I just felt like I had arrived at the top of my arduous ascent, and could enjoy the fabulous views. All that slog and effort could now be converted into a precious memory.

Give Me an Open Heart and a Boundless Future!

Suddenly I find that I have been here in Nepal for over a year. It has been an amazing process: I have taken a few hits, but learned many new things. Nepal is not the most advanced place on Earth, but I like to think of it as a great memory in the making. I have certainly experienced plenty of things I had never seen before I arrived. Sometimes the power cuts out halfway through dinner. We barely bat an eyelid, just carry on with our meal in the dark or by the light of a phone, chatting and laughing just as before. There are a lot of things you can't get here, particularly since the earthquake, so working out exactly what we should ask people flying in from China to bring us becomes a luxurious pleasure! We work hard out here, and I remember my mother once said to me, "If it's too much, just come back. We can take care of you here." But I have made my choice, and for me that's as good as a promise. I won't be a deserter!

I've also developed a fondness for hiking. It is another test of character: once you start a new route, there's no turning back. You have to follow the path through to the end. There may be people giving you a hand or showing you the way forward, but no one can carry you all the way to the summit. You have to make it there yourself. Youth gives us energy and bravado.

What I need to develop is the courage to face up to difficulties and to push through when the going gets tough.

When I'm old, I'm sure that I will look back on this time with fondness and gratitude for the time I spent in this little country with its power cuts and its seismic grumblings. "Gather ye rose-buds while ye may," as they say! I still have years to work here in Nepal, and lots more to learn. On the long road, I will keep on improving and growing. That's what we're supposed to do, isn't it?

Phewa Lake, Nepal

The 'Stubborn Bulldozer'

By Li Zhen

I never imagined
I would be described
like that. It is like
I am viewed as some
sort of superhero.

"Li Zhen? She's like a bulldozer."

"And I mean a real *stubborn* bulldozer."

That is how my two prior bosses would describe me to others.

"What do you mean?"

"Well just look at what she gets done. Almost no one can handle inventory management, but she gets it done. Also, look at the internal controls over financial reporting (ICFR). The Indonesia Office was at the bottom of the list in this regard. But she resolved the long overdue inventory issues, which made her famous. After closing the project, she didn't stop there. Instead, she decided to write a book. She is a force of nature, and is very stubborn. When applied to her work, this attitude makes her able to overcome even the toughest outstanding issues that no one else has been able to solve. She is like a bulldozer, ripping issues out of the ground, churning them up, and leaving no stone unturned from past projects in the South Pacific Region."

These descriptions are what I have heard through the grapevine about myself. I never imagined I would be described like that. It is like I am viewed as some sort of superhero. If you think about it, it's kind of cool. It's like you're playing a video game in real life. As you complete each task, your gear gets upgraded and your skills and fighting ability also increase. I guess personal growth is sort of like that.

Heading Out into the World with My Basic Gear

I joined Huawei in September 2012, working in the Working Capital Management Department as part of a team involved in inventory management. The team had only been established for four months, and was comprised of six senior financial experts from different parts of the company. Our goal was to get the company's global inventory management under control, make sure inventory could be verified, and ensure the books aligned properly with physical inventory. I was the seventh person to join the team, and was also the only new employee in the group.

After a year of learning, I began to feel as though I knew a thing or two. In September 2013, I went on a business trip to Indonesia. I was tasked with promoting standard actions in inventory management. This was the first time in my life I had left China. I never imagined that my fate would become so intrinsically linked to Indonesia.

The Indonesia Office had the worst global record for inventory problems. Its central warehouse recorded a shortfall of inventory totalling over US$30 million following stocktaking, with more than US$70 million in long overdue inventory. Even though the Indonesia Office knew there were problems, there was still a lack of awareness about inventory management. There was a pervasive view that this was an issue for the supply chain and delivery teams to handle, and that the finance team couldn't do anything about it. As a result, we ran into one issue after another when trying to promote new standards. Luckily for us, we had a very wise leader with the Project Financial Controller (PFC) team who gave me the opportunity to get more involved with each project and talk with each PFC. For over a month, I tried to put together a standard actions guide that was tailored to the specific circumstances in Indonesia. I wanted something that could provide guidance to PFCs on how to incorporate inventory management into their daily project operations management.

This was my first and earliest 'gear' to be put to use. I was full of confidence, and felt like I could almost taste success already. So I asked for approval from the CFO to get things rolling. But the CFO was sceptical: "What is the value of these standard actions? If we do these standard actions, will the inventory problems at the Indonesia Office be resolved?" This was the first time I had to present a report myself to a relatively high-level company leader. I was so nervous that my voice was shaking. Somehow, I was able to build up the courage to clearly explain the major inventory issues in important projects in Indonesia. I explained which problems could be jointly resolved by finance and the business side. I also emphasized how important this work was for HQ, and how great the expectations were for the Indonesia Office. I eventually convinced the CFO to sign and approve my request. As I clutched the approved document in my hand and strode out of that office, tears of joy started to stream down my face. So much emotion had built up in me leading up to that moment, and it all came flooding out.

I was deeply impressed by the can-do atmosphere of the frontline, and became inspired to work at the Indonesia Office. Unfortunately, this was easier said than done, due to budgetary restrictions and company policy. After nearly a year of hard work and patience, June of 2014 came around. It was at that time that I was finally re-assigned to the South Pacific Region as a 'Golden Seed' in inventory management. This marked the start of my re-engagement with Indonesia.

Li Zhen

Rising to the Status of Expert

I was greeted in my new role by a project for a local telecom operator. This project was a priority for company management because it ranked first in the region and among the top three globally in terms of the amount of long overdue inventory.

The amount involved approached US$30 million, and had been the subject of numerous reports. Supply chain and finance experts had previously visited the region to assist in the handling of the issue. Perhaps because they didn't stay for long enough, none of their efforts were long-lasting. The project team had therefore lost the confidence to address the issue and left it as it was.

I was the third Golden Seed to be sent overseas to the region. The first two Golden Seeds had failed to 'sprout' and had been relocated to receivables positions. I wasn't in any better shape than they were, and running into brick walls seemed to be the norm as soon as I started. It was next to impossible to obtain information about sales, no one responded to meeting invites, and the standard actions that had been launched locally a year ago weren't being followed. It was almost impossible to get things done. Although I was worried, I was fully confident that as long as I took the right approach, nothing could stop me. I decided to make a breakthrough by beginning with the PFC. I subtly relocated my work station to a place next to the PFC. This allowed me to listen in on the discussions the PFC was having with the project team, and, in particular, the daily work talk with the project manager. I gained a deeper understanding of the project in this way.

One day, I heard the project manager ask the PFC: "Wasn't that project closed a while back? Why are there still reports of inventory-related problems?" This got me thinking. I quickly pulled up the inventory data for that project and began studying it. Why was there still inventory in a closed project? What was the reason for that? It was easy to look up, and what I found was nearly US$200,000 in long overdue inventory. Was this my veritable 'foot in the door'? I suppressed the excitement welling up inside me, and steadied myself as I sought out supply chain staff, site engineers, and contract managers. I wanted to learn about the actual status of the physical inventory and site construction. I recorded and categorized all of the information that I was able to collect.

After more than a week, I finally had a good grasp of what was going on with this inventory. It turned out that there were nearly a thousand sites whose costs had not been correctly carried forward because records hadn't been made for material relocations between sites, and there had also been unauthorized distribution of materials during the construction. I sought out the project manager to explain the details, and his eyes widened in surprise upon learning about these issues. He immediately put me in charge of sorting things out. From there, I was able to coordinate with the Shared Services Center and the supply chain department to quickly sort out the inventory issue. This battle became the 'in' I needed to join the project team. They began to half-jokingly call me an 'expert'.

After that, the project manager sent me a data sheet for site construction containing hundreds of thousands of lines of information. There was long overdue inventory amounting to over US$20 million. This was the most difficult unresolved issue faced by the project team. It was their hope that I could help figure out a way forward. I spent half a month during the hottest days of summer rummaging through warehouses, visiting sites, verifying mountains of data, and double-checking everything. A picture gradually began to emerge: the borrowing of goods between projects and the inability to offset this had made it impossible to record revenue in the accounts. Records weren't made for re-allocation of goods between sites. At challenging sites, materials had been delivered, but then couldn't be installed and had gone missing. This gave me a good idea of what the problems were. The only issue left was, what to do about it?

To address the problems, it would be necessary to rope in multiple departments, including regional finance, accounting, contract management, and the Project Management Office. Cross-departmental communication was more difficult than I had imagined. I pulled everyone together at multiple meetings, but no one was willing to compromise. There would be plenty of verbal back-and-forth, but never any conclusions.

We couldn't keep on as we were, spinning our tires without any traction. Working with the project team, I wrote out all the problems the project faced, listed the pros and cons of each solution, and sent the details up through the chain of command to HQ for approval.

Finally, over the course of three months and a dozen meetings of various sizes, the project team and I were able to go through the approved solutions for several thousand individual contracts and tens of thousands of sites. Slowly but surely, we drove the execution of these solutions, and were ultimately able to clear up long overdue inventory worth nearly US$20 million, while recovering over US$60 million in revenue for the project team.

For me, the payoff was that my colleagues stopped joking about me being an expert. Now, I really was one. In the arcane field of inventory management, this Golden Seed took root in the South Pacific.

An Infographic that Went Viral

Only as I delved deeper into the field of inventory management did I realize that I was carrying more and more responsibility. I also had to continually upgrade my 'gear' to take on the challenges I was facing at these higher levels. In 2015, I added another light-weight piece of gear to my arsenal: an infographic giving a clear depiction of how physical inventory matches up with accounts.

At the start of the year, Ye Xiaowen, the Indonesia Office's CFO at the time, said that if we were to give the office a name, then it would be 'Alexander', which is a pun in Chinese that means 'Mountainous Pressure'. In 2014, the office received only 19 points in its ICFR assessment, ranking among the lowest of all the company offices around the world. The office had the dubious distinction of being named one of the 24 offices whose long-term improvements in internal controls had been 'unremarkable'.

With fire under our feet from HQ, who were pushing us to rectify the ICFR issue, we established a project team in Indonesia. I was appointed as the project manager. In collaboration with accounting, the business side, HQ, and the region, we uncovered and dealt with the various historical issues that involved ICFR. Issues we looked at included inconsistencies between physical inventory at base stations and accounting records as a result of the re-allocation of goods and unauthorized bundling of goods for quotes, non-compliant revenue and cost recognition, and irregular long overdue accounts receivable.

In early April, Li Hua, CFO of the South Pacific Region at the time, visited the Indonesia Office on business. After hearing a report from the accounts department with the most serious ICFR problem, he issued what turned out to be a critical order: the inconsistency issues in project N had to be resolved by the accounts department within a month's time. The constant manual adjustments to accounts had caused the inventory records in the supply chain system to be different from the inventory amounts in the finance system by over US$20 million. The direct result of this was to affect the consistency of the books with physical inventory for 20% of sites in the region. This was a top issue for the region if it wanted to achieve consistency of physical inventory and accounting records.

In 2014, we spent nearly half a year sorting out the long overdue inventory in the accounts department. Was it really feasible that we could complete the same for project N in a month? My heart was almost ready to jump out of my chest. We were backed into a corner with nowhere to run. There was nothing to do but roll up our sleeves and 'get'r done'. After the meeting that day, I immediately began an in-depth discussion with accounting colleagues. We eventually came to the conclusion that we would utilize internal contract changes to zero-out the inflated inventory caused by the manual adjustments to accounts. This would enable us to resolve the account variances in project N. With this approach, I stayed up all night to work on a plan with detailed steps outlining everything from delivery, finance, and accounting, to pre-sales, and everything in between. I made sure the responsibilities and to-do lists for each role were clearly defined.

Discussions relating to the review, decision-making, and actual implementation of the plan involved multiple layers of the organization, including the project team, the local office, the region, and HQ. Because the project itself was large (over US$300 million), and extended over a long period of time, there were a lot of records that just couldn't be located. HQ was requiring that we trace all projects so that there was evidence for each change that had been made. This meant that the frontline was in constant communication with HQ to clarify a wide range of matters. That month, we were either having a meeting or on our way to one. Issues became clearer the more we talked about them, and through our repeated discussions and debates, we knocked each of the 31 problematic contracts off the list one at a time. Each time we crossed one off our list, we would reduce the variance by several million US dollars, until we had finally cleared everything up.

After this, based on the experience we gained over those several months, I worked with accounting staff to develop an infographic on how physical inventory matches up with accounts.

Outstanding Team for Improvements to ICFR

The document provided important information on over 50 actions that need to be taken by five key roles, including prompt and accurate maintenance of budgets by finance, standardized quotes by the sales team, prompt and accurate triggering of revenue recognition by the contract and negotiation department, and standardized material collection by the supply chain department. I never imagined that after the infographic was released internally it would basically go viral. All of the offices in the South Pacific Region knew about it, and my colleagues from around the world began reaching out to me for the materials. It was really satisfying to receive that kind of recognition from everyone.

Receiving Recognition

Perhaps because of my history at the company of 'knocking out' tough problems, in 2016 I was sent to what we call at Huawei a 'Heavy Brigade' in project finance for the region. I was to be responsible for identifying and assisting in resolving major issues in the region. After less than a week in that position, I was sent to both Malaysia and the Philippines to assist the two offices in closing two outstanding projects.

I spent three months with a project team in Malaysia working to resolve issues relating to project changes. Then, in August, management sent me to support staff in the Philippines. The Philippines Office had been calling on the region to deal with these issues for quite some time.

As a 'firefighter', I had a lot of weight on my shoulders.

The Philippines Office ranked first in the South Pacific Region in terms of both long overdue inventory and inconsistency between invoice amounts and recorded revenue. The inventory turnover was also at the bottom of the pile globally. Based on past experience, it didn't seem like it would be too difficult. But the real difficulty lay in the fact that we ran into a new transformation program. The issues faced in Indonesia and Malaysia were more about the Integrated Financial

Services (IFS) transformation. At the risk of blowing my own horn, I was quite experienced in IFS. But S3, part of Huawei's Lead to Cash (LTC) transformation program, was new to me. It aimed to deploy the ERP system for project delivery. Back in 2014, the Philippines was selected as a pilot country for S3 and many issues had arisen during this process, which were left unsolved. My understanding of S3 remained abstract. As a result, in the first week of this new project when the project team told me about the issues they were facing, I didn't even understand what the problems were. There were too many specialized terms and I didn't know where to start. It was rough going.

I made a few calls to my two previous managers, looking for direction. They told me that if I really couldn't handle things, then I should just go back. But they also encouraged me to step outside my comfort zone, and to trust that eventually a breakthrough would be made. That advice made sense. After all, I had been able to clear up those tough inventory issues in the past. The challenges I was facing now were also something I could handle.

After this, I had meetings every day with the key people involved in the S3 project and colleagues who had the most challenging issues to deal with. In the daytime I sought out project managers to learn about project delivery acceptance. In the evenings, our team sorted through problems and studied S3 solutions. We almost always left the office after 11pm. Late in the evening when I was about to sleep, my mind would be swimming in data and how this data was generated. It was sometimes simply impossible to fall asleep, and I'd find myself with my eyes wide open right through until dawn. Each time the CFO of the office saw me, he would always comment on my raccoon-like appearance: "Don't get burnt out," he would console.

In my first month, I devoted myself to the project that had the largest influence on the inventory problem. I studied every contract of the project along with the project finance team, from order issuance to invoicing and payment collection, from product quotes to the bills of materials, and from shipments to acceptance inspections. We looked at every stage, every line of information, without exception. I roamed a sea of data, tracing the irregular data, and painstakingly investigating it. On numerous occasions I discovered non-compliant handling in the processes that the project team followed, and got into heated and red-faced arguments about the potential solutions with people in key roles. Incredibly, through those arguments, everyone came to a better understanding of S3 solutions, and gradually came to an agreement. After the solutions were implemented, we witnessed a gratifying result: the most troublesome project's long overdue inventory dropped by 40%. We were even able to contribute US$12 million in equipment revenue, and ICFR performance saw a marked improvement over July when the worst data was seen.

The issues connected to that most troublesome project were essentially resolved, but work to close out the project had only just begun. Project close-out is the last step of project management. For a long time, everyone's attention had remained focused on project acquisition and delivery. Project close-out was very easy to neglect. There were common problems such as unreliable information about site delivery status and missing delivery documents. And because no one had followed up on the issues for so long, it was extremely tough to reconcile the books with customers and every step taken to clear inventory was a hard slog.

That was basically what was being faced in the Philippines. We went to the customer to have them accept our work, but the customer told us that the sites hadn't been completely delivered. The customer had previously told us to cancel a portion of the sites, but the contract changes failed to keep pace with the latest agreements. After multiple changes to the contract, the contract information between us and the customer had become inconsistent. So we spent a full three months looking through the available site delivery proofs, and then went to the customer to ask them to accept our work so that we could issue them an invoice. We continually updated the data, found all of the proofs we needed for the contract changes, and encouraged company management to negotiate with customer executives to close out past projects as a whole. Once processes were streamlined internally, and a customer agreement had been received, we could quickly deal with the issues in our records.

In December, we finally received a letter informing us of project close-out, and we then promptly completed our internal processes to wrap things up. At the end of the year, the office's various metrics related to ICFR all showed a marked improvement, and our current month metrics were the best for the entire year.

My boss and colleagues were hugely supportive of me, and I received the recognition I felt I deserved for my hard work. My manager praised me, saying that since I'd visited the Philippines, internal control metrics had seen a significant breakthrough: things were finally showing signs of improvement. Days in inventory had dropped year-on-year by 92 days, and long overdue inventory had been cut year-on-year by over US$12 million, exceeding the stretch goal. We closed 43 projects, more than the goal we had set. The long-standing issues of invoicing and revenue variances had been essentially cleared up.

Perhaps because of my hands-on experience in Indonesia, Malaysia, and the Philippines, when I returned to the regional office, many PFCs came to talk to me about project close-out. Management suggested that I summarize my experience, and list out some commonly encountered issues. The handbook that eventually came out of those suggestions is now available as a first draft edition. I hope that it will benefit others in their work.

In 2014 when I was sent to the South Pacific Region, I shared a social media post that read: "If miracles really exist, they are just another word for hard work." Looking back on how I have grown over the past few years, I would say that I now believe in that phrase more than ever. I have worked with many very kind and very capable managers on my journey, and have received enormous help from so many colleagues within the company. I could write for hours about the happy and sad times we've had together. And the story will continue. There are more adventures ahead.

And with that, I'd like to leave you with a few inspirational words:

May the course of our lives be like a powerful river, streaming relentlessly onward, always and forever building in strength.

May our hearts remain undaunted as we pursue our dreams.

May we meet new friends as though living a song, and may our friendships be as strong as steel.

One Chip Connects Everything

By Zeng Chao

As a financial worker, I am good at making data 'speak'. But this story is about exactly how I, together with my colleagues, have done that.

Making things speak is a difficult process, but we persevered and finally succeeded in finding the best way to do this. It was like watching a baby grow: first crying, then babbling, then first words, and finally it manages to communicate.

"Where are you? Are you busy?" Though these are just simple questions, for us they are a big step forward in asset management.

Over the past three years, we have faced many difficulties in asset management. In the end, however, we managed to use a single chip to build up a huge asset management network with the Internet of Things (IoT), or asset IoT, across Huawei, and brought everything to life.

The Labour-Intensive Approach Came to a Dead End

"One asset booked under my name could no longer be found. I was told to pay almost CNY1,000 for it during stocktaking."

"Gosh, I have almost 100 assets booked under my name. I've lost track of some assets since they were lent to others."

"When I worked in a lab, all of the instruments were booked under my name. They were worth tens of millions of yuan. Every day crowds of people came to me to borrow the instruments. Each time we had to find all the different instruments during stocktaking. It really drove me crazy."

In June 2013, I transferred from the Financial Planning Department to the CAPEX Management Department. My job was to manage a huge number of company assets. I often heard employees complaining about asset management.

I totally understood why they complained. Huawei had more than 800,000 fixed assets booked under the name of its employees. That meant on average every employee had to manage three or four fixed assets, in addition to doing their own job well. The assets were moved so often between employees or departments that it was hard to keep track of them. Finding a single asset was like searching for a needle in a haystack.

Managing such an enormous number of assets was also no easier for our department. Annual stocktaking was like a marathon, and could take us up to six months. Even if all employees took part in this project, it was impossible for us to fully understand whether the assets were in use and under control. Asset losses and inventory shortfalls identified in each year's stocktaking were up to nearly US$3 million.

I realized that this traditional labour-intensive approach could no longer work because of its inefficiency and high cost. We had to explore a new, more effective way.

To this end, we held discussions with industry peers in China, consulting firms, the Huawei American Research Center, and other departments. But we found they were also at a loss as to how to effectively manage assets. During one casual conversation with Huang Chaowen, then the manager of the Financial Planning Department, we brought up asset management. He said, "Why don't you try IoT?" I was inspired. At that time, I was reading Kevin Kelly's *New Rules for the New Economy*. With respect to the management of a large number of parts, Kevin Kelly said: "The net is our future," and "Dumb parts, properly connected into a swarm, yield smart results." Wasn't he talking about the concept of asset IoT?

Project team members

With no help
coming from
outside, we
began to look
within instead!

Therefore, we established a project team to research the feasibility of the asset IoT solution. After some research, we found that the solution was viable. In the second half of 2013, we embarked on the journey of asset management with IoT.

Establishing a Large Asset IoT Network amidst Many Difficulties

Simply put, connecting assets with IoT is to make things 'speak' and give them the ability to proactively report their location and use status. Initially, we intended to buy mature IoT products. But after attending several exhibitions and checking all possible IoT products in the market, we found that none of them could satisfy our needs.

With no help coming from outside, we began to look within instead!

One day, my colleague Xi Yang excitedly ran back to the office, as if he had just discovered a cure for cancer. He loudly announced that he had found that company A's demo IoT product could be used for our asset management, explaining that the product had already been adopted in our manufacturing division.

Later, we found that the product used radio frequency identification (RFID) technology and had a built-in IoT chip. Our assets would be able to speak with this product. Like the human brain, the IoT chip could enable our assets to proactively report their location and use status. That meant the chip could instantly bring lifeless assets to life. This was exactly what we wanted. But could it serve our purpose?

The proof of the pudding is in the eating. So we immediately deployed 300 product demos in the Nanjing, Shanghai, and Shenzhen labs. The test results proved that the product had three killer features: automatic reporting, real-time monitoring, and remote management.

But the product also had obvious defects: oversized volume, limited use cases, short battery life, and high costs.

We naturally went to company A, hoping that they could improve the product and lower the price. But improvement was slow and we did not have the bargaining power to lower the price much. When the negotiations came to a deadlock, we realized that Huawei must establish and apply comprehensive, unified standards for products and technologies, so that we could introduce more partners on a fair, open basis. Ultimately this would improve product quality and cut purchase costs.

This is just like making clothes. If there is only one tailoring shop around, that tailor will be able to set the standards for the cloth, the style, and all other facets of production. You have no other choice but to buy clothes from that shop, even if they are not what you want, because you have no bargaining power. But if there are several different tailoring shops, you can request the cloth, size, and style and choose the shop that best meets your needs.

We were just bookkeepers, so how were we to develop the standards for 'making clothes'? But we didn't surrender. With concerted efforts from our colleagues in R&D and other departments, including Zou Guo, we finally made breakthroughs one after another. To solve the unit size problem, we went to the lab, and prepared foam models with a knife to explore the best exterior design. As for the poor battery life, we managed to push the limits as far as possible, extending the battery life from 1.5 years to 5 years.

In the end, we set the standards that we wanted for the 'cloth' and the 'style' – but still many of the 'tailors' didn't want to supply us. Some of them said they couldn't meet our standards; some of them said it would be a waste of time doing all that work for just one customer; and some were worried that we were trying to steal their technology and set up our own 'tailoring shop'!

After rounds of clarification, three 'tailors' agreed to give our 'clothes' a go. In the second half of 2014, we finally received the product. Because it followed our technical standards and communications protocols, its quality reached a new level:

performance improved by 50%, unit size was reduced by 67%, and cost was cut by 75%.

At the end of 2014, we began to install the IoT chip into our valuable assets. Making assets speak was not enough; we also needed a system to manage and apply the information reported, so then we developed the asset IoT system.

The system now manages 186,000 fixed assets, worth more than CNY14 billion. As the system matures, a large network that connects our global fixed assets is taking shape.

Finding or Borrowing Equipment No Longer Depends on Luck

After the asset IoT system was put in place, the assets reported their location and use status to the system. Employees could borrow or lend their assets with just one click and find their assets in seconds.

Not long ago, Liu from the Shanghai Research Center's wireless network product line was in urgent need of a special testing instrument to locate a network fault. But he didn't have the instrument and it would take at least three months to buy a new one. This was unrealistic, and he was very anxious.

"Go to different labs and ask everyone in each lab. If they have the equipment, you can borrow it; otherwise, you're out of luck." That was generally what he had been told when he had tried to find testing instruments in previous years. However, this time, the asset administrator told him to try the asset IoT system.

"Can I find the equipment by entering the model in the search box, just like on Taobao (China's largest e-commerce website)?" He visited the system, and found that he could conduct a fuzzy search based on model or description, and the results were displayed in order of proximity to his office and in order of low to high usage. He quickly found a model that was not in use, and submitted an application, asking to borrow the equipment.

Shortly after this, he got the equipment and successfully located the network fault.

Borrowing an asset no longer relies on luck, and finding the required assets is only a few clicks away. After taking a month-long vacation, one colleague in the Wuhan Research Center found his direct current regulated power supply worth US\$3,000 was gone! He nervously searched every corner of the building, but couldn't find it. He checked the Asset Management Tracking (AMT) system, but there were no records of it being lent out.

According to Huawei policy, he had to pay for the loss. Feeling disheartened, he remembered the device had a built-in IoT chip and it might help him find it. He immediately logged in to the asset IoT system. Surprisingly, he found that the power supply had been moved into another building. By following the directions in the system, he finally recovered his power supply.

Employees have truly benefited from the asset IoT solution. For departments that own many valuable assets, the solution has played a more effective role. Since the adoption of the solution, the R&D and manufacturing departments have been able to share over 1,000 assets, reducing costs on new equipment by CNY250 million.

'Marathon' Stocktaking Now Completes in Minutes

As an asset management department, we have found the IoT solution particularly beneficial. In the past, stocktaking felt like a marathon that took us several months to complete. Now it can be finished in minutes. Every year we can save up to 9,000 man-days in asset management, since tasks like stocktaking and preventive maintenance inspections are more efficient.

When I joined my department in 2013, they had just started annual stocktaking. At that time, the IoT solution was not in place and stocktaking was a real headache.

We had to send top-down notifications for the stocktaking, explain the policies and rules over and over again, and repeatedly remind employees to complete their end of the stock-taking. However, employees were either busy with their work or not in the office, and some of them had to spend lots of time finding their assets. All we could do was repeatedly urge them to complete the process as soon as possible. Those who failed to complete stocktaking were required to pay for their assets. Even with all this pressure, stocktaking was very slow and took more than six months.

Since we began using RFID in 2015, we have only required one person for this task, rather than needing all employees to pitch in. No rushing, no pushing; just a few flicks of the finger. After importing a column of asset numbers into the AMT system, we can complete the counting of 200,000 assets in a few minutes. Our efficiency has skyrocketed.

According to the stocktaking data in 2016, we reduced our manual workload by 53% because of the adoption of this IT system. The system is able to provide the most recent scan time and location of each asset, so we only need to manually count and check assets that cannot be found by the system. This both narrows down the scope of assets to be counted manually and improves efficiency.

In addition to reducing workload and saving time, the IT system significantly improves stocktaking quality.

With manual stocktaking, we were unable to control the quality of our process. For example, we had no way to know if employees were falsely reporting the asset information or lying about lost assets.

In order to prevent this, we had taken several initiatives. In 2014, we launched the Quality Stocktaking project, requiring all employees to provide photos of valuable assets during stocktaking. As a result, employees had to borrow cameras, apply to take photos of the assets, export photos from the cameras to their computers, and upload them to the system. All this work made stocktaking less efficient.

Now all stocktaking results are generated based on real-time data in the IT system, and we can be more confident about the results.

But this is not the end of our journey; it is a new beginning. As of right now, only half of our fixed assets, mostly located in asset-intensive areas, are connected. The other half are widely distributed, and we still have to rely on manual stocktaking. To connect all Huawei assets across the globe with IoT, we must first figure out how to connect the assets to the company's existing global network.

'Piggybacking' on Wi-Fi Enables 'International Roaming' for Company Assets

Internet connections are the basis for asset IoT. Without internet access, an asset is no better than a cell phone with no signal, no matter how many chips it uses. Huawei's fixed assets are distributed in over 180 countries and regions and the asset IoT network is independent from the company's existing global network. If we want to connect all assets around the world using IoT technology, we need to build an additional IoT network. Building and maintaining two IoT networks will require heavy investments in both people and money.

At one time, when we were thinking about how to connect worldwide assets, we found that the company had deployed more than 60,000 access points in our global workplaces to provide Wi-Fi coverage, and employees could automatically access Wi-Fi in any office they travel to. So why couldn't we exploit the company's Wi-Fi resources?

Then we began to consider using Wi-Fi equipment to provide data channels for RFID, so that RFID coverage would be available in places with Wi-Fi access. The company has already launched related read/write products, enabling an 80% cut in costs of access points in the asset IoT network.

Given the greatly reduced costs, we plan to expand this 'piggybacking' solution across the globe in the next year or two to ensure all assets are connected, as long as there is Wi-Fi coverage. By that time, the movements of all company assets will be under control.

Last April, I went to Spain for a business trip. We all know that Telefónica is based in Spain and has subsidiaries in countries like Brazil and Mexico. One asset administrator in our Spain Office told me that our colleagues there would often travel to the countries where Telefónica subsidiaries are located, so their assets would frequently move between Spain and other countries. The AMT system might display that their asset was in Spain, but actually it was in another country such as Brazil or Mexico. Although the assets were embedded with a chip, the Spain Office could not locate them if they were taken to areas that were not connected to the asset IoT network. So he asked how he could identify the location and use status of the assets in those areas.

"This won't be a problem if we get our asset IoT piggybacking on the Huawei Wi-Fi network around the world," I said. Once that happened, I told him, the assets would be visible no matter where they go.

This is the same with our cell phones: they can automatically connect to the company's Wi-Fi network in any of our offices around the world. In the future, our assets will also connect to the Wi-Fi network and be able to tell us where they are.

Wringing US$1 Billion Out of the Budget

By Wu Xiaohui

In 2012, the world economy was in bad shape. Huawei's telecom customers were not willing to invest, so the Carrier Business Group struggled to increase sales. The Enterprise Business Group was very new, and had not developed strong sales channels or found many named accounts yet. It had also over-invested early on, and was taking very heavy losses. The Consumer Business Group had only just shifted strategy to start developing high-end smartphones, and was also investing, but wasn't seeing any returns.

So in the first five months of 2012, we were operating at a loss, and our year-end sales turnover and profit targets were looking increasingly uncertain. At that moment, the Expense Management Department decided to step in. Supported by the company's three business groups and local offices, they developed a program to 'wring out' every penny of excess expenses. Ultimately they were able to make US$1 billion in savings, which made Huawei healthy profits, and kept poor cash flow from blowing us off our strategic course.

Wringing the Excess Out

On 6 January, 2012, I received an unexpected call from my manager. He told me that Huawei's sales growth was too slow, and expenses were too high. The department was locked in disagreement over the annual expense budget; that meant that our entire budget was behind schedule. Everyone was at their wits' end, so they wanted to know if I could be transferred to the Cost and Expense Management Department to help.

I had just been appointed the IT product line CFO – in fact, my appointment hadn't even gone through yet. I was rather worried at this sudden new assignment.

Up until that year, Huawei had experienced high-speed growth every year it operated. Our expense controls were fairly loose, and we had never had to make really big cuts to our budget. Now we were being told to 'wring out' excess expenses and cut down on spending. Inevitably, it was putting people's hackles up. To tell you the truth, I didn't really want to take on the job at first. But my boss said, "You don't have to carry this whole thing yourself. We'll go and sort it out together." I had worked in finance for many years, and had done cost accounting, been a product line CFO, and worked on the Integrated Financial Services program, a transformation program aimed at improving Huawei's financial operations. I had never been involved in expense management at the Group level before, but with the encouragement of my manager, I decided that I would give it a go.

But when I began work, I realized just how tough it was going to be.

A company's expense structure includes employee expenses, operational expenses, business travel expenses, overheads, and many other items which directly affect staff. Between 2009 and 2011, we had hired a lot of people, which led to a surge of fixed expenses. The 2012 expense budget was nearly 30% bigger than 2011's, but our revenue was only set to grow by 21%. We were projecting a big hit on our profit margins across the Group. With our expenses growing faster than our revenue, our budget work had ground to a halt, and so it was vital that we start cutting the fat.

When we took a closer look at each departmental budget, we immediately saw that budgets were ballooning fastest in the back-end functional departments. Some of them were having budgets rising at a rate of 45% per year. The Huawei philosophy is that functional departments should play a support role only, and that they should not have excessive budgets, headcounts, or authority over our frontline units. We are a 'small support platform' company, where most of the operational authority lies with the frontline teams. Because of this, we decided to start with the back-end functional departments.

When you 'wring' excess out of a budget, a department is forced to live hand-to-mouth throughout the process, so none of the departments were keen on volunteering to be first. We made calls to each of the functional departments to explain what we were doing, but it was hard work. Every department had a thousand reasons why it would be impossible to cut their budget. As a result, we weren't able to cut enough out, and on 12 March, the Executive Management Team (EMT), Huawei's most senior leadership team, rejected the draft budget that the finance department sent for approval.

Simply hacking off expenses wouldn't work. Wringing the excess out wasn't getting us anywhere. We needed to come up with a plan, with mechanisms and rules to ratchet our expenses down to size.

Baselines for Back-end Functions

Huawei had never had a systematic approach to expense budget management before, so we didn't have any existing practices to use. At a meeting of the senior finance team, the top finance management gave us some initial pointers. They told us to go and look at expense control practices across the industry, and to start to develop Huawei's own expense baselines and models.

Baselines are the third rail of budget management. If you set them too tight, the functional departments aren't able to keep up with growth, and that distorts operations. If you set them too loose, you eat into profits, making them grow slower than expenses.

We created separate expense baselines for each of the functional departments. For example, expenses of the business process and IT (BP&IT) department would make up no more than X% of company revenue. We also set figures for the functional department of each operating unit, i.e. the BP&IT budget for each region would be paid for out of that region's revenue, and so would be constrained by its financial performance. Expenses would not be allowed to grow faster than the region's sales revenue or gross profits. The rules for other functional departments at the headquarters were similar, adjusted for their individual situation.

These baselines gave us our first control mechanism, but we also developed another approach: absolute zero increase in expenses. We had been tasked with ensuring that our expenses did not grow faster than sales revenue or gross profits, but now the expenses were not allowed to increase YoY at all. We intended to starve our departments in order to make sure we wrung out every drop of excess spending. Of course, we received plenty of complaints, and met some resistance. But during the 2012 and 2013 functional department budget reviews, the rotating CEO and the CFO helped us, leading two reviews specifically of functional department expenses.

Every functional department now had to report its budget once again. At the meeting, the atmosphere was extremely tense. Faced with a zero increase in budget, all of the departmental budget reporters laid out their case for more money, and started competing with each other.

We analysed every department, every budget item, and over two review sessions, we whittled down the budget for the functional departments to US$66.39 million.

This gave us a basis for our expense budget for the functional departments. The Group Finance Management Department issued a series of regulations on expense budgets: *Functional Department Expense Budget Guidance, Cross-Charging Rules*, and so on. Finally we had gone from a complete lack of controls and authority to a position of having people and rules in place. Gradually, awareness that we needed to control our expenses spread through the company.

Flexible Budgets Forcing Us into the Black

Expense management was now moving in the right direction, and our spending was now all properly budgeted and accounted for. It seemed like we were set. But reality had a few surprises in store for us.

In early June 2012, after hearing the financial report for the first five months, the senior leadership of the company put this question to us: "We have made a loss every month from January to May. Do you think we can make a profit by June?"

The meeting room fell silent. No one dared predict that the first half of the year would end up yielding a profit; this was something that Huawei had never seen before, in all its fast-growing history. In the past, there may have been losses in January and February, but we could always drag the first quarter into the black with a push in March. We had never seen five consecutive months of losses, and no one was sure that a push in June would turn the situation around.

If our sales were not proceeding according to plan, then the only thing to do was to cut spending. More 'wringing' was needed, and thus we developed our flexible budget mechanism.

In theory, we had had flexible budgets for a long time but, as we had always been growing, they had only previously been used to increase budgets. No budget had ever been shrunk using the flexible budget mechanism, so we weren't sure it would be effective in practice.

In March 2012, as we were authorizing the budget for Q2, we had started to think about authorizing a flexible budget. As suggested by the CFO, the functional departments at the headquarters were only allocated 40% of their annual budget in H1. The profit centres would be required to link their budgets to their revenues, and would be also granted a flexible budget.

In June, under pressure to tip the company back into profit, the company took stricter control over flexible budget authorization on major profit centres. A flexible budget would be granted up to the level of their revenue or gross profit (whichever was lower). If they were not hitting their planned business targets, then their budgets would go down. To give an example, if a certain region had completed 95% of its annual sales targets, but was only hitting 90% of its gross margin targets, then only 90% of its budget would be granted and 10% of its budget would be cut away. This rule was imposed on all accounts departments, business groups, and country offices.

This method helped us bind resource allocation tightly to output indicators, and forced our profit centres to pursue not just revenue but also healthy gross margins.

Once this rule was in place, our department would make quarterly reports to the members of the Finance Committee (FC) about which departments had exceeded their budget. They would then have to come and explain to the FC members what had happened. In cases of serious budget overrun, we would remove their authority to sign off on their own expenses. The CFO also got the EMT to order that immediate hiring and pay-raise freezes be placed on departments that exceeded their budget, and overrun expenses be recouped with funds from the department's bonus package.

We now had clear flexible budget authorization rules, and strict processes for implementing them. The effect was immediate! The regional offices and business groups which would possibly miss their annual revenue and gross profit targets according to the mid-year forecast results started voluntarily reviewing their own budgets and cutting down on expenses.

By 2012 year end, Huawei had only completed about 90% of its sales and gross profit targets, but we had also controlled the expense budget to 90% exactly. We had wrung about US$1 billion out of the budget, and our end of year profits were in line with expectations. We had also put a stop to the runaway expense growth of the previous few years.

Managing Our Managers' Sign-offs

As the flexible budget rules grew stricter, we still discovered quite a lot of fake expense claims and petty fraud. For example, in one Muslim country it was very rare for locals to eat Chinese food, but we found a suspicious number of receipts from Chinese restaurants. Moreover, the claimed amount was more than the amount that a dinner would reasonably cost in a Chinese restaurant. When we investigated, it turned out that these were falsified expenses.

So how were we to control this process to prevent excessive expenditure or falsified expense claims? First, we updated our expense policies for business travel and working with contractors. This gave us regulations that we could rely on when trying to stop false claims. The Huawei business travel expense policy had been drafted in 2007, and had not been updated for five years; during that time, China had built an entirely new high speed rail network. In 2012, we updated and optimized the policy.

Next, with the help of the Accounting Management Department and the FC Office, we started to filter out and identify all of the false claims. We focused on the entertainment claims, wrote new regulations on entertaining customers and released the baselines for business travel expenses. That same year, the company's disciplinary committee, part of the HR Committee, approved the request from Finance that expense fraud be included in the Business Conduct Guidelines, Huawei's code of ethics for its employees. As a result, a whole system for checking and enforcing real expenses was set up.

Our investigation revealed that the discretion of the expense approver was the key control point when employees were submitting expense claims. Would the approver sign off on them? This was the main hurdle that an expense claim had to clear.

However, many managers wanted to get expenses out of the way quickly, so they did not check the claims very carefully. Most managers never looked at the receipts themselves, just clicked the button in the system, and all sorts of personal expenses ended up being claimed.

We handled this by conducting an analysis, and began to manage our managers' sign-offs.

In our analysis, we found that 104 managers had a compliance rating of C, and our net caught one very big fish. A senior executive was found to have a compliance score of just 42/100. He had not checked if the claims he approved were real or reasonable, and as a result, the company suspended his authority to sign expense claims. The suspension lasted three years, and he was held jointly responsible for paying back all the improperly approved expenses.

When his suspension was published, it was a wakeup call for every expense approver in the company. Everyone realized that they had to use their authority over expenses properly, and better manage their team's expense claims.

After further research into the practices in local offices, we produced a series of policies and regulations on expense approval, so that every responsibility centre had authoritative rules to rely on.

Distinguishing Strategic Investments

The three tactics we mentioned above showed how to save money, but our fourth effort focused on exactly how we should spend our money: allocating resources in a specific way based on their expense type, rather than just allocating funds in whatever way helps meet short-term KPIs.

1 – Separate budget for strategic investments

At the beginning of 2012, Huawei started to invest more in fundamental research and management transformation projects. That year was not a great year for sales, but cutting the funding for these projects would have serious impact on the company's long-term growth and development.

To make sure that strategic investments weren't impacted by short-term market difficulties, we separated the annual operating budget from the strategic investment budget. We developed a list of strategic investments which were separately funded and accounted for. This funding came directly from the Group, and there was a regular review to ensure that it was being properly followed up on. Any department which failed to follow through with these strategic programs would be named and shamed. That ensured that the company's strategies could be implemented.

2 – No scrimping and saving on customers

When budgets were tight, some departments would start to scrimp on customer engagement and customer entertainment. They found all sorts of ways to save a little here and a little there. As part of our customer-centric orientation, we divided up internal and customer expenses, and asked everyone to wring the excess out of internal expenses first. With the company's baseline in place for customer spending, we told teams not to try to squeeze too much out of customer expenses. We also broke each category down further to make sure that the customer budget was not sneakily reassigned to internal uses.

To be more effective, we got a new company regulation passed to the effect that savings could not be kept in the same department. That meant that if a team did save money on their customer interface, that money could not be used for internal overheads. Nothing must be allowed to distract us from business development and customer experience. With this new system, we got the excessive expense cuts we needed in overheads, but customer spending was protected.

3 – Dividing operational expenses
from personnel expenses

I remember one executive reminded us that Huawei employees are not spring onions. With spring onions, you plant more in the good years, and pull them in the lean years. But cultivating a good manager is a three- to five-year process. So we divided our operational expenses from our personnel expenses. We spent time talking to HR about the best way to handle personnel expenses, and how to do more longer term planning for company staffing, while operational expenses would be scaled up and down depending on the revenue that a department achieved that year.

We also made a separate list of expense accounts for contractor services, and flexibly linked the budget of these expenses to the amount of outsourced business or output.

4 – Negotiations: responsibility centres
VS resource departments

Responsibility centres are responsible for their own financial performance. Inevitably, they don't want too much responsibility loaded onto their shoulders. Resource departments have to deliver services to the business departments, and develop the skills of their staff members, so they also do not want to live hand-to-mouth. At the time, everyone used to complain about how slow and expensive the BP&IT department was to complete a project. But the BP&IT department thought they were the victims, because their internal customers kept changing the parameters of their orders.

We needed to cut through this Gordian Knot: a transparent internal mechanism, wherein both departments would sign a cross-charging agreement. The responsibility centre would clearly budget its need, and the resource department would have a basis on which to prepare the resources necessary. Prices were set at price hearings by third parties, or by the HQ department which coordinated the relevant function. That was the best way to ensure fair, objective pricing.

Conclusion

In 2012, Huawei missed its annual sales target for the first time ever. That year our growth was the slowest it had been in a decade (only 10% YoY), and our gross margins fell. We made only 90% of the gross profit projected in our 2012 annual budget.

Luckily, the company had seen the risk coming, and quickly took action with the flexible budget and other resource allocation measures. The expense controls in each department were also very impressive and well-targeted. Together, we 'wrung' US$1 billion out of the budget, and every penny of that meant more profit for Huawei. At the same time, we didn't cut strategic investments or customer spending, which laid a solid foundation for our robust growth in the years to come.

Editors

Biography
of Tian Tao